Social Media Livestreaming

Social Media Livestreaming: Design for Disruption? addresses a host of emerging issues concerning social media livestreaming, exploring this technology as a disruption and its potential to shape journalism practice and influence society.

Live visual images increasingly inundate our digital screens. While once restricted to broadcast news organizations, "going live" is becoming ubiquitous, fueled by smartphones and social networks. As livestreams and eyewitness video permeate our social media feeds, a wide range of possibilities for journalism and society are unfolding. Using international case studies, interviews with journalists, and survey research with citizens, this book explores major themes including livestreaming's implications for journalism practice and news content production; citizen activism and participation in democracy; ethical, legal, safety, and privacy considerations; and the role of livestreaming in shaping public perception.

Social Media Livestreaming: Design for Disruption? is ideal for multiple audiences, from academic researchers to professional journalists and social media practitioners as well as policy-makers and organizations.

Claudette G. Artwick is Associate Professor of Journalism and Mass Communications at Washington and Lee University, USA.

Disruptions: Studies in Digital Journalism
Series editor: Bob Franklin

Disruptions refers to the radical changes provoked by the affordances of digital technologies that occur at a pace and on a scale that disrupts settled understandings and traditional ways of creating value, interacting, and communicating both socially and professionally. The consequences for digital journalism involve far reaching changes to business models, professional practices, roles, ethics, products, and even challenges to the accepted definitions and understandings of journalism. For Digital Journalism Studies, the field of academic inquiry which explores and examines digital journalism, disruption results in paradigmatic, and tectonic shifts in scholarly concerns. It prompts reconsideration of research methods, theoretical analyses, and responses (oppositional and consensual) to such changes, which have been described as being akin to "a moment of mind blowing uncertainty."

Routledge's new book series, *Disruptions: Studies in Digital Journalism*, seeks to capture, examine, and analyze these moments of exciting and explosive professional and scholarly innovation which characterize developments in the day-to-day practice of journalism in an age of digital media, and which are articulated in the newly emerging academic discipline of Digital Journalism Studies.

Geographies of Journalism
The Imaginative Power of Place in Making Digital News
Robert E Gutsche Jr. and Kristy Hess

Disrupting Journalism Ethics
Stephen J. A. Ward

Social Media Livestreaming
Design for Disruption?
Claudette G. Artwick

For more information about this series, please visit: www.routledge.com/ Disruptions/book-series/DISRUPTDIGJOUR

Social Media Livestreaming
Design for Disruption?

Claudette G. Artwick

Routledge
Taylor & Francis Group

LONDON AND NEW YORK

First published 2019 by Routledge

2 Park Square, Milton Park, Abingdon, Oxon OX14 4RN
605 Third Avenue, New York, NY 10017

Routledge is an imprint of the Taylor & Francis Group, an informa business

First issued in paperback 2022

Publisher's Note

The publisher has gone to great lengths to ensure the quality of this reprint but
points out that some imperfections in the original copies may be apparent.

British Library Cataloguing-in-Publication Data
A catalogue record for this book is available from the British Library

Library of Congress Cataloging-in-Publication Data
A catalog record for this book has been requested

ISBN: 978-1-138-58639-0 (hbk)
ISBN: 978-1-03-233870-5 (pbk)
DOI: 10.4324/9780429504617

Typeset in Times New Roman
by Apex CoVantage, LLC

To all the truth seekers who livestream on social media.

Contents

Acknowledgments

My deepest gratitude goes to Bob Franklin, *Disruptions* series editor, for making this book possible. Many thanks to Scott Eldridge II for his guidance on the digital journalism handbook chapter that was foundational to this work, and to Kitty Imbert and Jennifer Vennall at Routledge. I also wish to thank Autumn Spalding and the team at Apex CoVantage.

Lenfest Grant support and a Washington and Lee University sabbatical afforded me time to research and write, for which I am grateful. I extend my sincere appreciation to the professionals at Leyburn Library, and to the scholars, journalists, and livestreamers whose work I cite. Warmest thanks to my Reid Hall colleagues, and to friends and associates, for sharing thoughts, expertise, and kindness.

And I am enormously grateful for my family's love and support. My heart is full.

1   The disruptive force of live social video

It's night and he stands in the street in darkness. We see his face, wearing a neutral, hollow expression. "It's a horrible thing," he says. "Nothing like this should ever happen. Ever!" Hiding in a classroom just hours before, David Hogg lived through a massacre at his high school in Parkland, Florida, where a gunman with an assault weapon killed 17 people. And now, only steps away, Hogg is livestreaming the aftermath (2018a).

On the border of Columbia, thousands of Venezuelans are fleeing their country. "We're dying of hunger," a woman cries, gesturing toward her young children and husband. Carlos Arturo Albino, a reporter for Noticias RCN, livestreams the exodus on *Periscope* (2018).

In southern California, a wall of flames fills another livestreamer's screen, as wildfires sweep through the hills near Los Angeles. "That's the blowtorch effect," the narrator says, as a towering evergreen explodes in flame. Fire photographer Tod Sudmeier is talking to 10,000 viewers, responding to comments and questions as he averts flying embers (2017).

These scenes and countess others have made their way onto digital devices across the globe – emblematic of the "raw and personal moments" Mark Zuckerberg envisioned livestreaming would bring (2016). *Facebook Live*, *Periscope*, *YouTube*, and other social media platforms have propelled live broadcasting into new territory, far beyond the once exclusive realm of television. A space that historically transmitted unidirectional messages to a passive audience now offers interaction, eyewitnessing, and personal perspective. The lines blur between journalist and citizen, participant and observer, turning what were once lecture-like broadcasts into engagement. This is social media livestreaming. Its content flows through our feeds and digital media platforms, allowing us to bear witness, to participate, and more.

While this valuable tool holds promise, it comes with a price – the danger of harmful behaviors and effects. Livestreams offer drama and distant witnessing, but at the same time, can reveal unspeakable horror. In many ways, live video streams bring the potential for disruption.

This chapter explores that potential by examining a major news issue through the lens of social media livestreaming. The mass shooting at Marjory Stoneman Douglas High School in Parkland, Florida, and the survivors' #NeverAgain movement have garnered extensive news coverage and a multitude of livestreams, making it an ideal case for analysis. By examining the many facets of this social media form, its use, and potential effects, the chapter probes its potential as disruptor – in both the negative sense and as a positive force for change.[1] And it introduces guiding concepts for understanding the technology and its social and cultural impact.

Livestreaming and #NeverAgain

The images and sounds you may remember from the Valentine's Day shooting are likely graphic – bodies on the floor, the SWAT team, gunshots, screams. And gripping – lines of teens walking with their hands up, parents waiting anxiously, tearful embraces. Those moments, captured by students and others on the scene, were infused into live news coverage, on both television and social media. *Facebook Live* broadcasts were abundant, streamed not only by Florida TV stations, but by national and international media, like Australia's 7 News Sydney (2018).

Many news organizations simply fed their live television coverage onto social media platforms, but others were instantly interactive. A *Twitter* initiative positioned Miami's *WSVN-TV* broadcast in a livestreaming window adjacent to the timelines of its U.S. users (Kantrowitz 2018). Not only did this open the event and the graphic images to widespread viewing, but it provided a venue for comment and conversation both on *Twitter* and within the *Periscope* app. The story immediately included discussions of gun control, terrorism, and school safety, even before the suspect had been taken into custody.

Some viewers shared the news on their social networks as a live broadcast-within-a-broadcast by pointing their phones at their TV sets. Others livestreamed themselves on camera, discussing gun violence and terrorism. *Ask an Imam* used *Periscope* to condemn the shooting (2018). "Regardless of the identity of the person who is carrying out this act . . .," he said, "We show our voice, we stand up to gun violence."

On the scene, a bystander streams from an underpass near the school. Several police officers come into view, and one asks, "Did you barricade the door?" (@Grumpyhaus 2018). Thousands watch these *Periscope* streams, including journalists seeking permission to include them in their own coverage. The livestreamer grants it by announcing, "Anybody can use my images."

As day becomes night, on-the-scene coverage continues. Bright lights illuminate journalists' live shots outside the school. And while they labor, Stoneman Douglas student journalist David Hogg goes live, too, right alongside them.

Using *Periscope*, he shows viewers the crime scene tape and TV news crews. When he flips the view towards his face, blue-white light from a nearby squad car streaks by, creating an eerie moment. "It's awful," he says, shaking his head, lips tensing into a frown. "It's not OK" (2018b). In another stream, he denounces the shooting: "It is something that should never have happened, and nobody should ever have to witness" (2018c).

But as witness to tragedy, Hogg's live video stands out among the multitude of livestreams on the Valentine's Day mass shooting. It's personal and unfiltered, coming from just outside the building where his classmates died. It's dark and gritty. And it signifies the role and power of live social video, holding potential for disruption. In these early livestreams, he takes a step toward activism, announcing that "This is a problem in America. This is a problem that needs to stop here" (2018a).[2]

As he streams on *Periscope*, others on the scene take notice, and approach him. "Do you want to say something?" a voice off-camera asks. "You can ask me some questions," says Hogg. "I'm livestreaming it, though" (2018b). After a few minutes he closes the app and then appears on network television.

Two nights later, Hogg goes live with classmates on *YouTube* (2018d). And in a separate *Periscope* stream, they ride together in a car, grappling with what happened in their school. He invites viewers to join their conversation. "If you guys have any questions, just comment, we'll answer them" (2018e).

The response is almost immediate, and focuses on guns. "Teachers need to be armed to prevent shootings," comments @johnartist3.

Hogg reacts, "If you think teachers need to be armed to prevent shootings, that's your opinion and I respect that. I respect everybody's opinion out there and I respect the right of other people to disagree with that." A voice from the back seat says, "I would be more afraid of my teachers if they had a gun. Because I'm already afraid of them as is."

Along with the gun control discussion, emotions bubble up. A classmate tells the story of her escape, holding a flower she received for Valentine's Day. "The entire time we were running away I was holding onto that stupid carnation, and eventually it broke. But I was basically denying all the stuff that was happening." After she saw the helicopters, she said she knew it was serious, and thought, "I might die today." But she didn't cry right away. That came after she heard about a friend who had been shot. "It still doesn't feel real. It just feels like I'm in a really bad nightmare, you know."

After streaming for 48 minutes, Hogg closes with, "Get some laws passed to prevent the next mass shooting. Because there's another one coming. God knows where it is, or when it's going to be. But we've got to start working towards ending it now. Children's lives depend on it" (2018e).

These streams offer a rare glimpse into the thoughts and emotions of teens as they process a traumatic life event. Unlike filtered interviews with reporters, the unvarnished stories come directly from the survivors during their private, yet concurrently very public, conversation.

The next day, students, teachers, and parents rally for gun control in Fort Lauderdale, Florida, and millions watch livestreams of their speeches and video-clipped sound bites. A young woman in a buzz cut takes the stage. Wiping her eyes, fighting back tears, Emma González pauses for a moment of silence (2018). And then, she calls out politicians for taking money from the NRA, and the crowd joins in, "Shame on you, shame on you, shame on you!" She continues revving them up, "They say that tougher gun laws will not decrease gun violence. We call BS!" The emotion escalates as she shouts, "They say that no law would be able to prevent the hundreds of senseless tragedies that have occurred." The crowd thunders back, "We call BS!" (González 2018).

González, Hogg, and other Stoneman Douglas survivors become the faces of a movement, #NeverAgain. "We are going to be the kids that you read about in textbooks, not because we are going to be another statistic about mass shootings in America, but because . . . we are going to be the last mass shooting" (González 2018). The next week, they make a trip to Tallahassee for another rally and to meet with state legislators. Later in the day, invited students attend a listening session with Donald Trump at the White House. Others appear in a Town Hall on *CNN* with legislators, law enforcement, and Dana Loesch of the NRA. All these events are streamed live.

A journalist at the Tallahassee rally found one speech especially moving. "It gave me the shivers," said Andrew Kimmel, who was livestreaming for *BuzzFeed News* (2018a). Afterward, at the airport, he clipped the video and tweeted several sound bites from Sheryl Acquaroli's "Dear Congress" speech:

> Who will die next because of your lack of action? Who will you murder next? Because your lack of action is causing people to die. The next person who dies because of an AR-15 will be on YOU . . . !
>
> (Acquaroli, in Kimmel 2018b)

Kimmel's clips and others from the day's events traveled through social networks, along with links to the full recorded broadcasts. Repurposing and sharing livestreams can increase their reach and impact. It's all part of a process called *flow*.

Flow as a guiding concept

In *The Inevitable*, Kevin Kelly draws insight from his years at *Wired* magazine to predict how technology will shape the future (2016). Kelly says we're entering an age of computing in which flows and streams replace pages and browsers. In this era he calls the *Flows*, some of these streams exist only in the moment, flowing past in real time. And it's the real-time expectation that relates to the flow. "Unless it occurs in real time, it does not exist," argues Kelly. And, "in order to operate in real time, everything has to flow" (64).

Kelly's concept of *flow* can be applied to social media livestreaming. Not only do livestreams unfold in real time, but they can be digitally manipulated – key components in Kelly's model.

He explains that digital manipulability, or copying, contributes to the flow through "the number of ways a copy can be linked, manipulated, annotated, tagged, highlighted, bookmarked, translated, and enlivened by other media." What matters, he argues, is "how well the work flows" (74).

And social media livestreaming *flows* exceptionally well. Even if we don't watch in real time, livestreams can, and do, reach us via *flows*. The many forms include:

- Social media alerts with embeds or links to the live videos in real time.
- "Timestamps" shared from *Periscope*, sending viewers to key moments in the feed.
- Embedded clips from the live video in tweets or posts.
- A clip from the live video in a TV news story on the air.
- An online digital photo, grabbed from the live video in a screen shot.
- A published photo (hard copy newspaper or magazine).
- A screen shot still frame in a TV news broadcast.
- A clip or still frame featured on a TV talk show or entertainment program.
- An image on a poster or flyer.
- An audio clip from the live video used in a radio report or podcast.
- Related livestreams made by people commenting on the live video.
- Tweets, shares, snaps, and other social media referencing the live video content.

And outside the digital realm, we may hear about the live video in person from friends, family, and others in our daily lives. Content can flow in the other direction as well, incorporating pieces of media from other sources *into* the livestream. For example, during the mass shooting at Marjory Stoneman Douglas High School, a student made a video inside a classroom and posted it to *YouTube*. Soon, television journalists included that video in their own coverage, which was going out in real time on other social platforms.

These *flows* become part of our cultural storytelling.

School walkouts and the road to March for Our Lives

As plans for the March for Our Lives solidify, celebrities including Oprah Winfrey, George and Amal Clooney, and Steven Spielberg vow to donate millions of dollars to the cause (Khatchatourian 2018).

By late February, more than a dozen companies severe ties with the NRA, ending discounts and special services for members (Fortin 2018).

And Dick's Sporting goods stops selling assault-style rifles (Siegel 2018).

The Parkland students continue speaking out, appearing on television and online. Their social media followings burgeon. And they tweet deftly. A study reported in *The Washington Post* showed that Stoneman Douglas students dominated the gun conversation on Twitter. The 12 accounts examined produced nearly nine times the conversation of other top tweeters on guns (Fowler 2018).

Their tweets facilitate information dissemination, propelling the movement forward. Livestreams and clips become part of that *flow*. For example, after a protest in Washington, D.C., on March 7, 2018, Hogg reaches out on Twitter for news about the event.

> To the teens that got arrested for peacefully protesting outside Mitch McConnell's office today I haven't been able to find out much more, are you guys ok? If anyone finds a link to a news story about them please post it
>
> (2018f)

Recording artist Ricky Devila tweets a link to a *Periscope* livestream and Hogg retweets it, adding, "PEACEFUL PROTEST can, has and will bring change AMAZING JOB guys #NeverAgain #MarchForOurLives" (2018g). Within a week, the *Periscope* video made by independent journalist Alejandro Alvarez had nearly 1 million views (Alvarez 2018). The livestream became the *flow* – watched in real time, saved, and shared on social networks.

Just weeks after the shooting, Florida lawmakers pass a bill to change the minimum age to buy a gun from 18 to 21, ban bump stocks, and create a waiting period. While they don't ban assault weapons, the measures are the first changes to gun legislation in 20 years (Astor 2018). The governor signs the bill into law, despite his concern about its controversial provision to allow teachers to carry weapons (Mazzei 2018).

Exactly one month after the Stoneman Douglas massacre, gun control remains on the national agenda. With past school shootings, the issue had dropped off significantly over time, in a "ritual of tears, recrimination and political stasis" (Barabak 2018). But on March 14, 2018, students from nearly 3,000 U.S. schools perpetuate the momentum as they participate in class walkouts, joining in solidarity with Parkland survivors to protest school shootings and advocate for gun control (Yee and Blinder 2018). Social livestreaming, again, brings these demonstrations onto screens worldwide. They carry symbolic images for the lives lost – balloons released, empty desks, teens "lying-in" – as hundreds of thousands of students march on streets and sidewalks, tracks and football fields, shouting the mantra, "enough is enough!"

News organizations are in the air and on the ground covering the walk-outs, feeding live on *Facebook*, *Periscope*, and *YouTube* to millions of viewers.[3] Students stream their own events, as do adults and organizations. Some hold up their phones for only a few moments. Others broadcast for 17 minutes (for the 17 lives lost), and longer. Much of the teen content is ephemeral or privately shared in snaps and *Instagram* live videos.[4]

But public snaps do appear on an interactive heat map display, Snap Map (2018). Because students post snap videos essentially as they are made, the map content emulates a livestream. As the 10 a.m. start-time crosses into each time zone, new snaps appear and exude the teens' energy and excitement. This student-generated content becomes part of mainstream news coverage, with *The New York Times* and others embedding screenshots of the map into their stories to illustrate the magnitude of the walkouts.

At the same time, adults are streaming live using *Periscope* and *Facebook*. In Chicago's "Back of the Yards" neighborhood, an enthusiastic group marches, shouting, "What do we want?" "Peace!" "When do we want it?" "Now!" Then, a chilling moment of silence honors the lives lost to gun violence there, with 20 shootings in the first three months of 2018 (Aguayo 2018).

Politicians host their own streams – Nancy Pelosi on *Periscope* and Bernie Sanders on *Facebook*. And that very afternoon the U.S. House passes a bill to increase school security and safety training with more than $50 million in funding (Lambert and Lynch 2018).

As the March for Our Lives (2018) approaches, Parkland students travel to *Twitter* headquarters in New York City for a live Q&A. The host reads questions tweeted to the hashtag, #AskMSDStudents, including "What advice would you give a seven-year-old who wants to change the world?" and Kim Kardashian's tweet asking, "Has this experience made you want to run for office?"

March for Our Lives

The day of the march finally arrives, and more than a million people take to the streets (Hayes, Jackson, Collins, and Dastagir 2018). Again, social media livestreaming is there – around the world – to tell the story. From the March for Our Lives' own finely polished production, to teens going live on their favorite platforms, streams become the *flow*. Riding along in a bus, teenager @evilemilie reaches thousands of viewers on *Periscope* (2018). She holds a Deer Park water bottle like a microphone and sings, "The struggles I'm fa-cin'. The chances I'm ta-kin'. Sometimes might knock me down, but, no I'm not brea-kin'." Eyes on her screen, she sees, "Where are you heading?" and stops mid-verse, shouting, "Going to March for Our Lives in D.C., whooooo!"

Just a few hours later, Miley Cyrus is singing those same lyrics on stage at the rally. In a grey MSD-strong hoodie, she holds a NEVER AGAIN sign, as her fans join in, "And I. I gotta keep try-in'. I gotta keep my head held high" (*NBC News* 2018).

Celebrities and children energize and inspire. "I have a dream that enough is enough," says Yolanda Renee King, the granddaughter of Dr. Martin Luther King Jr. She leads the crowd in a trio of chants, and before the third, shouts, "Now I'd like you to say it like you really, really, mean it, and the whole, entire world can hear you! Spread the word! Have you heard! All across the nation! We! Are going to be! A great generation!" (*NBC News* 2018).

Livestreaming and human connection

March for Our Lives, both in real life and via livestreams, offered participants and viewers a common experience, a means for us to connect. In her book, *Braving the Wilderness*, sociologist Brené Brown writes about the importance of human connection through shared experience. "Show up for collective moments of joy and pain so we can actually bear witness to inextricable human connection" (Brown 2017, 120).[5]

Sharing moments collectively – such as the joy of a wedding or the pain of a natural disaster – can bring us together, writes Brown. She advocates for connection through in-person experiences. But one could also argue that social media livestreaming can play a role in human connection, through the interactive nature of live comments and the collective emotions shared in watching an event as it unfolds in real time.

The #NeverAgain movement has given us collective moments. "These kids are making me proud of my country again!" posted a viewer on the March for Our Lives *Facebook* livestream (Hayes 2018). Both collective joy and collective pain can be seen in events surrounding the massacre at Marjory Stoneman Douglas High School. Just days after the shooting, viewers empathized with Emma González while she spoke at a rally in Fort Lauderdale. As she fought tears and called "BS," viewers wept, and also felt hope and promise. In one of myriad livestreams, comments illustrate the shared emotion (*WPLG* 2018).

Bryce: *These kids have me in tears. Happy tears. I know that when I'm old. They are gonna be doing the right things.*

Angele: *She is a next leader. With tears in my eyes I'm sending strength to all whose suffering.*

Sabrina: *This girl is amazing. Thank God she will be a voter sooner than later.*

Randi: *I am so proud of this generation of leaders!!!!*

Carrie: *Her passion is amazing!!!*

Moving forward

As the Parkland students graduate and move on to the next chapter in their lives, gun control remains on the national radar. Social media livestreaming played a role in the *flow* that brought this tragedy and the activism that followed to the public conscience. By the end of May 2018, two-thirds of Americans favored banning semi-automatic weapons (*Reuters* Polling 2018). And, during that same time frame, 44 gun safety bills in 23 states had been signed into law (Giffords 2018).

Yet, school shootings persist – eleven in just three months post-Parkland, with ten people killed at Santa Fe High School near Houston, Texas, alone (Cox et al. 2018). But if David Hogg and the Parkland students have their way, "The young people will win" (2018h).

For the uninitiated: the nuts & bolts of social media livestreaming

What is it?

Live broadcasting using a smartphone* and a streaming app. Viewers watch on their digital devices, such as phones, tablets, and laptops. *Facebook Live*, *Periscope*, and *YouTube* offer livestreaming that can be seen by the public, and can be saved and searched, for later viewing. *Instagram* and *Snapchat* live broadcasts are more restrictive.

Twitch is primarily a video game streaming service, but also offers pop culture content.

How to find livestreams?

Users can view interactive maps on *Facebook Live* and *Periscope* to see live broadcasts in real time. They can also search within the apps. Streamers also send notifications to followers when they go live.

What's social about it?

Engagement. Viewers can comment in real time during the livestream, to communicate with the broadcaster and others watching the broadcast. They can also send hearts and other emojis to show their support, depending on the platform.

Connection. When broadcasters go live, people in their social networks can receive notifications for instant connection.

Types of livestreams

Planned event – Rally, news conference, town hall, panel.

> *Creator*: The livestreamer creates the event and livestreams it, to make an announcement, release information. These streamers are generally businesses, political figures, celebrities, or government agencies (such as police). Interaction with virtual viewers can vary, but often does not take place.
> *Participant*: The livestreamer is on-site at the event. The production may take a number of formats. Unfiltered: the scene unfolds in front of the camera with no narration. Filtered: the streamer narrates both on- and off-camera. May or may not communicate with people at the event, or with commenters.
> *Observer*: This can be a journalist or nonconventional journalist. It can take place on the scene, or virtually. Communication with virtual viewers ranges from turning off comments to full engagement.

Breaking event – Crash, accident, attack, shooting, natural disaster (fire, storm, earthquake).

> *Victim or on-scene eyewitness*: Person who was on the train that derailed, whose home was hit by a tornado. May narrate and/ or communicate with commenters.

Observer: Journalist or other. Come to the scene to report, or happen upon the scene and want to share it.

Chat format program – The livestreamer is the host and chats with the commenters.

Gaming – From Twitch "About" page:

> "Welcome to a community where millions of people and thousands of interests collide in a beautiful explosion of video games, pop culture, and conversation. With chat built into every stream, you don't just watch on Twitch, you're a part of the show. From classic TV show marathons to esports tournaments, if you can imagine it, it's probably live on Twitch right now." Interestingly, a first-person shooter game is featured prominently at the top of this page, under the headline, "Don't just watch, join in."
>
> (Twitch 2017).

Getting started

With *Facebook Live*:
https://live.fb.com/about/

With *Periscope*:
https://help.pscp.tv/customer/en/portal/articles/2003640-how-do-i-broadcast-

With *YouTube*:
https://support.google.com/youtube/answer/2474026?hl=en

* Note that media organizations and brands often use professional video cameras to livestream.

Notes

1 Margaret Sullivan, media columnist for *The Washington Post,* used the term "force for good," when writing about *Facebook Live* exposing police violence in Minneapolis. She cited Diamond Reynolds' livestream after police shot Reynolds' boyfriend, Philando Castile, as "an important piece of bearing witness" (2017).
2 For Hogg, "Action is therapeutic." In his book, *#NeverAgain*, co-authored with his sister, Lauren, he wrote about going back to the school that night, and his earlier interviews with classmates during the shooting, "I knew I was doing the best thing I could, so I just did my job and pushed the rest of it out of my mind. Not consciously, almost like an instinct" (Hogg and Hogg 2018, 97).

3 The news livestreams attracted a total of more than 6 million views by late after-noon the day of the march, 3/14/18. Searches for "walkout" conducted between 4 and 5 p.m. yielded 4.3 million views of the livestreams on *Facebook,* 1.9 million on *Periscope*, and 104,000 on *YouTube*.
4 A recent study found *Instagram* and *Snapchat* to be the top social media plat-forms for teens (AP/NORC 2017). Hence, I searched Instagram the following morning. Search terms: #walkout yielded more than 83,000 posts, #neveragain yielded 1.3 million, and #enough yielded 1 million. However, the search did not reveal which videos had been livestreamed.
5 Brené Brown's concepts of collective joy and pain draw from Emile Durkheim's *collective effervescence*, from his book, *The Elementary Forms of the Religious Life*, 1912.

References

7 News Sydney. 2018. "7 News Sydney 7 news breaking." *Facebook Live*, February 14. www.facebook.com/7newssydney/videos/2006237272733729/

@evilemilie. 2018. "On our way." *Periscope*, March 24. www.pscp.tv/evilemilie/1DXxyXLAqnZJM

@Grumpyhaus. 2018. "@coralspringsfl @stonemandouglas." *Periscope*, February 14. www.pscp.tv/Grumpyhaus/1MnxneqbbDmJO

Acquaroli, S. 2018. In Kimmel 2018b.

Aguayo, B. 2018. "#IncreaseThePeace walkout in back of the yards!" *Facebook Live*, March 14. www.facebook.com/berto.aguayo1/videos/vb.100001704030478/1637950092938443/?type=2&video_source=user_video_tab

Albino, C. A. 2018. "Frontera con Venezuela." *Periscope*, February 12. www.pscp.tv/CarlosArturoAR/1rmxPmZOEBgKN

Alvarez, A. 2018. "I'm LIVE from Capitol Hill where students are sitting-in on Mitch McConnell's office for gun reform." *Periscope*, March 7. www.pscp.tv/w/1mnGeXPBpYLKX

AP/NORC. 2017. "Instagram and Snapchat are most popular social networks for teens: Black teens are most active on social media, messaging apps." *The Asso-ciated Press-NORC Center for Public Affairs Research*. www.apnorc.org/PDFs/Teen%20Social%20Media%20Messaging/APNORC_Teens_SocialMedia_Messaging_2017_FINAL.pdf

Ask an Imam. 2018. "Muslim response to High School shooting #Parkland #Gun-Control." *Periscope*, February 14. www.pscp.tv/w/1BRJjrNaWgoJw

Astor, M. 2018. "Florida gun bill: What's in it, and what isn't." *The New York Times*, March 8. www.nytimes.com/2018/03/08/us/florida-gun-bill.html

Barabak, M. 2018. "It's been a generation since Congress passed a gun control law: Will young protesters change that?" *Los Angeles Times*, February 22. www.latimes.com/politics/la-na-pol-school-shootings-guns-20180222-story.html

Brown, B. 2017. *Braving the Wilderness: The Quest for True Belonging and the Courage to Stand Alone*. New York: Random House.

Cox, J., Rich, S., Chiu, A., Muyskens, J., and Ulmanu, M. 2018. "More than 215,000 students have experienced gun violence at school since Columbine."

The Washington Post, May 25. www.washingtonpost.com/graphics/2018/local/school-shootings-database/?utm_term=.f057bbec8ed2

Fortin, J. 2018. "A list of the companies cutting ties with the N.R.A." *The New York Times*, February 24. www.nytimes.com/2018/02/24/business/nra-companies-boycott.html

Fowler, G. 2018. "They survived a school shooting only to wage battle in some of the nastiest corners of the Internet." *The Washington Post*, March 8. www.washingtonpost.com/news/the-switch/wp/2018/03/08/the-parkland-survivors-are-children-remember-that-when-they-go-viral/?utm_term=.ab58ae338e26

Giffords. 2018. "Pressure leads to progress." *Giffords.org*, June. https://giffords.org/pressure-leads-to-progress/

González, E. 2018. "Gun control rally." *Facebook Live, WPLG Local 10*, February 17. www.facebook.com/WPLGLocal10/videos/10155291675278837/

Hayes, A. 2018. Comment posted to "March for our lives." *Facebook Live*, March 24. www.facebook.com/marchforourlives/videos/1637975672946937/

Hayes, C., Jackson, D., Collins, A., and Dastagir, A. 2018. "At 1 million plus strong, March for Our Lives rallies make powerful statement." *USA Today*, March 25. www.usatoday.com/story/news/2018/03/24/march-our-lives-hundreds-thousands-expected-rally-across-u-s/430245002/

Hogg, D. 2018a. "Douglas high school Parkland FL." *Periscope*, February 14. www.pscp.tv/davidhogg111/1vOGwALDAkMxB

Hogg, D. 2018b. "Parkland FL shooting." *Periscope*, February 14. www.pscp.tv/davidhogg111/1djGXdbDOgkGZ

Hogg, D. 2018c. "David Hogg was live." *Periscope*, February 14. www.pscp.tv/davidhogg111/1YqKDdvOjbVKV

Hogg, D. 2018d. "Students of Marjory Stoneman Douglas high school two days after the reaction." *YouTube*, February 16. www.youtube.com/watch?v=Pb0MKcZpbzs

Hogg, D. 2018e. "Students react to Douglas massacre." *Periscope*, February 16. www.pscp.tv/davidhogg111/1mrGmRVanrwJy

Hogg, D. 2018f. *Twitter*, March 7. https://twitter.com/davidhogg111/status/971582301686718464

Hogg, D. 2018g. *Twitter*, March 7. https://twitter.com/davidhogg111/status/971587845277306880

Hogg, D. 2018h. *Twitter*, May 30. https://twitter.com/davidhogg111/status/1001947329212092417

Hogg, D. and Hogg, L. 2018. *#NeverAgain*. New York: Random House.

Kantrowitz, A. 2018. "Twitter's Marjory Stoneman Douglas high school livestream was part of a new initiative." *BuzzFeed News*, February 14. www.buzzfeed.com/alexkantrowitz/twitter-live-local-news-broadcasts-timeline?utm_term=.gj6PWAkNx#.sdWj4KPRV

Kelly, K. 2016. *The Inevitable: Understanding the 12 Technological Forces That Will Shape Our Future*. New York, NY: Penguin Books.

Khatchatourian, M. 2018. "Clooneys, Spielbergs, Katzenbergs, Oprah donate to Parkland students' March for Our Lives." *Variety*, February 20. http://variety.com/2018/biz/news/george-amal-clooney-donate-parkland-shooting-1202704831/

Kimmel, A. 2018a. Telephone interview with the author, March 9.

Kimmel, A. 2018b. *Twitter*, February 21. https://twitter.com/andrewkimmel/status/966431059721244672

Lambert, L. and Lynch, S. 2018. "School safety bill passes House, no action on gun control." *Reuters*, March 14. www.reuters.com/article/us-usa-guns-legislation/school-safety-bill-passes-house-no-action-on-gun-control-idUSKCN1GQ26R

March for Our Lives. 2018. *Twitter*, March 19. https://twitter.com/AMarch4OurLives/status/975775920815472640

Mazzei, P. 2018. "Florida governor signs gun limits into law, breaking with the N.R.A." *The New York Times*, March 9. www.nytimes.com/2018/03/09/us/florida-governor-gun-limits.html

NBC News. 2018. "March for our lives: A rally to end gun violence | NBC News." *YouTube*, March 24. www.youtube.com/watch?v=NKb7mW4YSJA

Reuters Polling. 2018. http://polling.reuters.com/#!poll/PV21B_3/type/smallest/dates/20180223-20180309/collapsed/true/spotlight/1

Siegel, R. 2018. "Dick's Sporting Goods CEO says company will stop selling assault-style rifles, set under-21 ban for other guns." *The Washington Post*, February 28. www.washingtonpost.com/news/business/wp/2018/02/28/dicks-sporting-goods-ceo-says-company-will-no-longer-sell-assault-rifles-guns-to-people-under-21/?utm_term=.7f403aa0f910

Snap Map. 2018. Screen shot of map from *Snapchat*, March 14. https://support.snapchat.com/en-US/a/snap-map-about

Sudmeier, T. 2017. "#CreekFire 4." *Periscope*, December 5. www.pscp.tv/w/1nAKEWVQdzoJL?q=epn564

Sullivan, M. 2017. "Facebook still denies what it is: The Cleveland murder shows how." *The Washington Post*, April 18. www.washingtonpost.com/lifestyle/style/mark-zuckerberg-has-vowed-to-limit-live-streamed-depravity-so-far-its-an-empty-promise/2017/04/18/d44de158-243c-11e7-b503-9d616bd5a305_story.html?tid=ss_tw&utm_term=.93e690747c01

Twitch. 2017. "Don't just watch, join in." *Twitch About Page*. www.twitch.tv/p/about/

WPLG. 2018. "Gun control rally." *Facebook Live*, March 17. www.facebook.com/WPLGLocal10/videos/10155291675278837/

Yee, V. and Blinder, A. 2018. "National school walkout: Thousands protest against gun violence across the U.S." *The New York Times*, March 14. www.nytimes.com/2018/03/14/us/school-walkout.html?smid=tw-nytimes&smtyp=cur

Zuckerberg, M. 2016. "Live video launch." *Facebook Live*, April 6. www.facebook.com/zuck/videos/vb.4/10102764535989511

2 Livestreaming as a journalistic tool

Your feed opens to a sea of hot pink "pussyhats" and signs reading "#Time's Up" and "Vote in 2018." People are chanting, "Hey hey, ho ho, Donald Trump has got to go," as they march out of Logan Square in Philadelphia.

"I'm doing this for my two-year-old," says a young mom carrying a toddler on her shoulders. "Her rights are what I'm fighting for today, and what I'll be fighting for tomorrow."

The live broadcast switches to New York City where reporter Michael Nigro is interviewing Whoopi Goldberg. "Vote what you believe and then you stand tall," she tells viewers.

Next, you're in Washington, D.C., in the midst of a crowd – again, marching. A child's voice calls out, "Tell me what democracy looks like!" The crowd shouts back with fervor, "This is what democracy looks like!" (*BuzzFeed News* 2018a).

It's the Women's March 2018, and these are some of the scenes *BuzzFeed News* is livestreaming on *Facebook* and *Periscope*. For more than five hours straight, reporters on the ground take you to five different locations. Behind the scenes in New York City, journalist Andrew Kimmel managed the coverage. "We want to give viewers a frontline experience," he said. And that means going beyond the static television liveshot. "With livestreaming you give the power to the viewer to determine what they've seen. Unedited content is the closest thing to being there" (2018a).

For Kimmel, witnessing is a major driving force behind live video. "Especially in this era of fake news," he says (2018a). Live social video makes it possible to witness protests, civil disobedience, and police standoffs as they unfold. In the days following a Confederate statue-toppling in Durham, North Carolina, Gloria Rodriguez of *WTVD* reported live on *Facebook* (2017). In one of several livestreams, she follows police down a hallway as they escort protesters in handcuffs to a room she is not allowed to enter. One of the officers says, "At this point we're entering a secure part of the facility, so you guys have to stop here, OK." The door slams and she keeps the camera rolling through the wire-enforced glass window. The portability of her phone allowed her to livestream on *Facebook* and offer witnessing in real time to thousands of viewers (2017).

After police fatally shot an unarmed black man, Stephon Clark, in California, Frances Wang of *ABC10* streamed the protests that followed. We see her marching along as the *Periscope* stream opens, "Hey everyone. We are here in Sacramento on I-5." She flips the view to the crowd, "They have shut down the freeway here. There are hundreds of protesters marching." We hear them shouting as she pans the crowd, "Whose streets? Our streets!" The video attracts nearly a half-million views (Wang 2018).

By livestreaming in the field, journalists can provide credibility and truth telling. "A fiction can be heard or told, but a fact is witnessed" (Peters 2001, 720). As John Durham Peters wrote, "Liveness serves as an assurance of access to truth and authenticity" (719).

Early livestreaming in journalism

Some of the earliest adopters of the technology used it during Occupy Wall Street (OWS), before *Facebook Live* or *Periscope*, when Tim Pool and Henry James Ferry teamed up to broadcast live on *Ustream* (Lenzner 2014). OWS began streaming with just one roving camcorder, a laptop, and a 4G wireless card (Captain 2011), finding ways to circumvent barriers and problem-solve. From marches to arrests, the streams brought the movement to viewers worldwide.

Then in March 2015, *Twitter* launched *Periscope*. Among the 1 million people who joined in the first ten days (Rodriguez 2015), journalists came on board and soon began using the tool in their reporting. Paul Lewis of *The Guardian* was an early adopter, interviewing presidential candidate Rand Paul live on *Periscope* in May (Lewis 2015a). And when violence broke out in Baltimore following the death of Freddie Gray, Lewis opened up the app to stream from the streets.

As the live broadcast begins, Michael Jackson's "The Way You Make Me Feel," is blaring on a loudspeaker. Lewis walks along, narrating what he sees unfolding in his path. Bottles are smashing nearby as he says, "It's definitely not (pause) feeling very safe here right now." But he stays calm and holds steady during what sounds like a shot nearby (Lewis 2015b).

He continues streaming as he talks with people he encounters along the way. Things get tense as he begins an interview and his subject looks decidedly nervous. "Oh, oh, oh, oh," the man says as he pivots to protect two young girls in pink coats standing behind him. "Bring the girls back this way, bring the girls . . . come, come, come," you can hear Lewis as they turn to run, and the camera cuts out (Lewis 2015b).

In another broadcast, tear gas invades the scene, and Lewis senses it's time to stop streaming. "I'm going to check out, this is getting really dangerous," he says (Lewis 2015c). Despite the hazards, Lewis says there's an advantage to working alone without bulky equipment and a crew. "You can kind of melt into the crowd." It allows you to give people an "unvarnished perspective on what's happening" (Lewis, as quoted in Artwick 2018). Experience and core training give journalists the foundation for livestreaming during a volatile situation. "You're applying the same journalistic principles to the new technology," he said (Lewis, as quoted in Artwick 2018).

In the months following the uprising in Baltimore, livestreaming continued to bring the human side of news to light. After the body of a Syrian toddler washed ashore on a Turkish beach in September 2015, a burgeoning refugee crisis was becoming evident. Other journalists broadcast the volatile situation emerging in the Middle East and Europe live on social media. As thousands fled Syria and other Middle Eastern countries, journalists walked alongside the migrants as they attempted to cross international borders. With their portable, relatively unobtrusive smartphones, correspondents could show the struggle with video and, when feasible, livestreams via *Periscope*. Among them was Paul Ronzheimer of the German newspaper, *Bild*. As he traveled across Europe with a group of Syrian refugees – from the Greek Island of Kos to Germany – he used his iPhone to broadcast live interviews and key moments throughout the journey (Dredge 2015). He later created a documentary from that footage (*Bild* 2017). *Al Jazeera English* (2015) livestreamed Q&As on *Periscope* with correspondent Mohammed Jamjoom. And photographer Patrick Witty (2015) Periscoped refugees landing in Lesbos, Greece, for *BuzzFeed News*.

Journalists later adopted *Facebook Live* to cover the refugee story. In July 2016, Andrew Kimmel livestreamed on *Facebook* from inside the Skaramangas refugee camp in Athens, Greece. It was a way to "engage people from another culture," he said (2018a).

Challenges in the field

Engagement sets livestreaming apart from one-way TV broadcasting. But working in this interactive and potentially volatile environment can present challenges for journalists. During the Baltimore unrest, Lewis encountered a constant stream of unfiltered postings, noting that the "really inappropriate comments" were his biggest challenge. "You have people being extremely racist, using the fact that you have this audience to propagate fake news or false rumors. The bubbles of text were disappointing and alarming" (Lewis, as quoted in Artwick 2018). He responded in his narration by calling out what he saw as inappropriate and warned viewers he would turn off the comments.

Kimmel reflects on one of his early *Periscope* broadcasts. There was a standoff between police and protesters at the Los Angeles International Airport after Trump's first travel ban, and the comments were fierce. "It felt like I was part of the Hunger Games," he said. "It was so bizarre that people were engaging with this content and taking a side" (2018a).

Back at the Women's March in Philadelphia, livestreamer Lauren Sorge transitions seamlessly between narrating, talking with marchers, and reaching out to viewers. She does this all while managing to keep up with the crowd, albeit at times a bit breathlessly. "If you have any questions or comments please write them in the comment section. I'll do my best to answer" (Sorge 2018).

The *Facebook* comments on that stream are overwhelmingly positive. But the trolls venture out as well, especially on *Periscope*. Sorge does not acknowledge them. On some feeds, commenters patrol the trolls. "Go away trolls and Russian bots!!" writes a viewer, as nasty comments appear during Michael Nigro's interview with filmmaker Michael Moore (*BuzzFeed News* 2018a). Kimmel says that troll factories are an issue, but noted that *BuzzFeed News* was not blocking comments (2018a).

Beyond managing comments, a range of other challenges face journalists who livestream in the field, like moving through crowds. As Sorge walks along, her camera framing briefly goes awry, and she quickly catches herself, "Almost tripped. Hahahaha. You guys didn't witness that, but I almost just tripped and fell on the ground" (2018). Walking backwards while broadcasting is just one of many challenges, especially when working alone. Solo livestreaming is fairly standard practice. It often requires holding a monopod in one hand and microphone in the other while navigating the crowd, monitoring the stream, and watching what's unfolding around you. "It's a very stressful and tenuous job," says Kimmel, "because on top of all that you could be in the line of fire, or risking arrest." In Charlottesville in August 2017, "We had rocks and bottles flying overhead and bear mace sprayed in our faces," he recalls. Another journalist got clipped by the car that drove into the crowd, says Kimmel. "It got one of his cameras" (2018a).

Amidst violence, there's the potential to livestream while someone is being brutally attacked, or at the moment of death. "It's a fine line between showing people the reality of the situation and trying to respect viewers and whoever the family might be," says Kimmel (2018a).

Aerial photojournalist Stu Mundel often faces volatile situations as he livestreams from a helicopter above Los Angeles. During a standoff near City Hall in Long Beach, California, Mundel stays zoomed out for most of the broadcast, narrating throughout as a man stands outside a white van holding what appears to be a gun. "It is a very serious situation," says

Mundel. "One of the things that he's been threatening and talking about is that he's got explosives inside his van" (2018).

After nearly an hour, while still on the wide shot, the man appears to turn toward the van. There's a flash, and he falls to the ground. A SWAT vehicle drives up and a dog runs into the frame and attacks the man's body on the ground. After a few moments, Mundel warns viewers, "If you guys are watching live now, this might be one of those times when you *don't* want to be watching, because apparently they may have shot that person" (2018).

Some of the viewers are stunned, while others ask to see more. As the man is wheeled away on a stretcher, they comment (Mundel 2018):

Brittney: *Wow he's dead.*
Astrid: *Close up-close up close up.*
John: *I just watched someone get shot live. What a world we live in.*
Holly: *They shot him live on FB.*

Grave outcomes can also follow other tense situations, like high-speed chases. "My biggest fear is always that somebody is really going to get hurt or die or there's going to be, you know, some extremely innocent person injured," said Mundel (quoted in *CBS* 2017).

But not all livestreams in the field focus on breaking news or violence. Many of *The New York Times*' broadcasts on *Facebook Live* feature performing artists – from a choreographer rehearsing a ballet at London's Royal Opera House, to singer Joan Jett, of "I Love Rock 'N Roll" fame. Jett's livestream at the Sundance Film Festival attracts nearly a half-million viewers. The *Facebook* page encourages interaction with Jett. "Leave your questions for her in the comments, and NYT journalist Mekado Murphy will ask some" (Murphy 2018). Murphy begins with his own questions, and then segues to some from viewers. The shot stays trained on Jett throughout the 16-minute livestream, framed head-and-shoulders, aligned to reveal the tattoo encircling her upper left arm. She looks at Murphy while he asks questions, then directs her responses to her audience, looking directly into the camera lens. "Nothing's changed," says Jett about women in music, and in "every facet of society." She says, "If anything, it's worse in a way. Because people are led to believe that we're liberated." Jett references the #MeToo movement without naming it, saying, "It's time for that to be discussed" (Jett, in Murphy 2018).

That same weekend, women rallied worldwide. But *The Times* did not livestream the 2018 Women's March – unlike the previous year, when its live interactive coverage was a large-scale production from multiple locations.

Louise Story managed the 2017 Women's March coverage, and was the journalist "face" on *The Times*' webpage. Her photo and title, Reporter and

Executive Producer, Live Interactive Journalism, appeared in the right margin, at the top of the comment section. She likened the production to a scaled-back TV control room, with a team of four people working in-house (Artwick 2018). But unlike TV news, the journalists were also communicating with viewers around the world who posted their questions on the live comment section of *The Times'* website and via *Facebook*. Story's introductory comments invite viewers to participate: "Welcome Everyone, this live video chat is here for you to interact with our reporters in the field at these protests. I'm here to guide you through what we're seeing. Ask questions here and I'll answer some and steer some to the people you see in the live video!" (*The New York Times* 2017). In order to do that, she communicated with correspondents in the field around the country by text, email, and cell phone (Artwick 2018). Story said the team was well-equipped to answer questions, having covered the election for months. One technique that helps reporters in the field, she said, is the "pinning" feature. The person in the newsroom who is monitoring user comments can post a question at the top and keep it there by pinning it. That way, when reporters on the ground glance at their phones, they can see the question of interest right up top (Artwick 2018).

Journalists streaming live can also face technical challenges in the field. If the crowd is competing for an Internet connection, there may be dropouts, or simply no connectivity. Kimmel says, "The biggest issue is always the connection." Spending time, money, and resources to get to a location, and then not being able to connect, is "very frustrating" (2018a). That happened in Oklahoma City, where thousands of teachers were protesting. Kimmel tweeted, "There are so many people here that signal is practically non-existent – unfortunately we can't go live #Oklahoma #okteacherwalkout" (Kimmel 2018b). Their workaround involved posting videos and still photos of the protest, and they were eventually able to stream by going inside the state Capitol rotunda (*BuzzFeed News* 2018b).

Static locations with reliable Internet service are sometimes the only options for livestreaming. Some news organizations choose to bypass crowds and action and set up on the outskirts of an event in exchange for that security. However, it's a trade-off that risks missing a major development that might break in the thick of the crowd. Livestreaming from the studio is another option.

Interactive studio livestreams

Broadcasts coming straight out of TV studios fill *Facebook Live*, *Periscope*, and *YouTube*. Some are completely unidirectional, essentially feeding a television newscast onto a social media platform for viewing. Others open comments to viewers, generally unfiltered and unmoderated. But the truly interactive studio livestreams have adapted their newscasts, moderating the discussion with viewers in the livestream as the newscast unfolds. The *CBC* streams its nightly hour-long news program "The National." Its March 5, 2018 broadcast on *Facebook Live* is interactive even before the program begins, with the moderator welcoming viewers in the comment section (*CBC* 2018a).

> *Happy Monday everyone! Did you have a good weekend? Let us know how it was and where you're watching from tonight.* ^ml

Viewers respond from Kuala Lampur, Portugal, the United States, and all over Canada. As the screen counts down to the broadcast – 49, 48, 47 – the livestream moderator posts again.

> *WARNING: Our lead story tonight contains a graphic image of an unidentified man believed to be dead.* ^ml

> Kane: *Thanks for the warning! BTW what do we call you ML?* :)

The moderator responds, but doesn't share his/her name:

> *CBC* News: *Hi Kane, I'm the moderator of the livestream* :) ^ml

As the newscast continues, the moderator posts links to the stories being covered and includes questions for the viewers.

> *CBC* News: *In a rare move on Monday, Toronto police released a photograph of an unidentified man who investigators believe is another victim of alleged serial killer Bruce McArthur.*
> *www.cbc.ca/1.4561794* ^ml

During the first segment, which runs about 25 minutes, there are at least 20 comments, many interacting with viewers. That engagement is no accident. "We want to be part of the real-time conversation," says Senior Producer Irene Thomaidis. She's in the "nitty gritty of livestreaming every day," and tells a roomful of journalists at ONA 2017 that preparation is key to a successful *Facebook Live* broadcast (Thomaidis 2017). Before the newscast, an associate producer prepares a document with information related to the newscast, like links to stories, and they break it down block by block. "To follow along with the real-time conversation you can't be looking for links," she says (2017).

This interactivity has paid off over time. "We have built a really interesting connection with the audience," says then-*CBC News* Senior Director Brodie Fenlon, also at ONA 2017. "We want to engage." Although these are smaller audiences, they're loyal, and serve as a kind of focus group on their programming, says Fenlon (2017). Its *Facebook* page shows views for the program in the 40,000 range, and exceeding 100,000 for the livestream following the fatal van attack in Toronto (*CBC* 2018b).

Live, interactive story forms like these illustrate some of the essential dimensions of what Kovach and Rosenstiel say define journalism as service or public dialogue (2010). They do so by providing a forum for discourse where citizens are empowered as participants.

Other newsrooms have turned to this story form during breaking news. When word of a shooting at Central Michigan University emerged just a few weeks following the Parkland, Florida massacre, *WILX News* 10 in Lansing, Michigan, streamed live from its newsroom on *Facebook*. In this very fluid situation, the viewer is almost part of the reporting experience as it happens, witnessing the behind-the-scene newsroom activity and contributing by posting to the *Facebook* page.

Throughout hours of coverage anchor/reporter Joe Sam reports live updates and responds to viewer comments, such as "Michelle wants to know, who are the deceased?" he reads. "We're getting in confirmations that the two people who are deceased are those of the shooter, the parents of the shooter," he reports as he points to the suspect's photo on a large video monitor (*WILX* 2018a).

Sam also interacts with his colleagues, walking over to the producer's desk for updates, and weaving others into the coverage. At one point, a female journalist comes into the frame and holds up her phone to share a conversation she's having with a source (*WILX* 2018b).

He also pauses to listen to other journalists in the newsroom as updates come in. "Some people are saying that he was a junior at the university, but . . . we're still tracking that information," he says. A woman off-camera says something, and he's quiet for a moment. He then makes the confirmation and addresses the *Facebook Live* viewer who posted a question, "So, to answer your question Mr. Antione, he is a student at the campus" (2018a).

Social media livestreaming is also bringing the radio studio to the interactive audience. On Saturday mornings, Scott Simon opens his *Periscope* app to viewers before his Weekend Edition show on *NPR*. Donning a sweatshirt (or, on occasion, T-shirt and jean jacket) he stands behind a gigantic microphone, adjusting his headphones and multi-tasking. His vibe is casual and conversational with the *Periscope* viewers and his producer, yet highly professional when going live on the air. On the St. Patrick's Day broadcast, as he's lamenting about not wearing any green, he glimpses a post from the Emerald Isle, and immediately responds, "Well, greetings from Ireland! Good morning! I know it's not such a big thing there, right? That's what my mother used to tell me. It's mostly ours – particularly in Chi-CAH-gee" (Simon 2018). As he prepares to record the week's essay, he suddenly coughs loudly to clear his throat, and fiddles with his script and stand. He then takes a sip from a black mug and starts reading his script. "Rashid is the name of a man in a photo that was seen around the world this week." After recording, he checks the comments, and jokes with someone who posts, "What a soothing voice."

In the two years that Simon's been livestreaming from his *NPR* studio, his *Periscope* audience has grown from a couple of hundred to upwards of 10,000 viewers. While not in the millions, like the on-air show, the livestreams give listeners a chance to see the man behind the microphone, and even interact with him. And they share their appreciation (Simon 2018):

@just_jotter: *Highlight of my week watching these live vids!*

Forum for discussion

Livestreams also give the public a venue for discussing key issues. Even streams with little or no interaction with the reporter or news organization provide this space for conversation among viewers. This has become an important function in a news marketplace where the commenting feature has been removed from stories and online news platforms. *NPR*'s own website discontinued comment sections in late summer 2016, joining a list of other news operations that have shut down comments, including *The Chicago Sun-Times*, *Reuters*, and *Popular Science* (Jensen 2016; Ellis 2015). And more recently, *The Atlantic* shuttered its comments section after, it said, robust conversations were increasingly "hijacked by people who traffic in snark and ad hominem attacks and even racism, misogyny, homophobia, and anti-Muslim and anti-Jewish invective" (Goldberg 2018). A new Letters section aims to elevate the discourse: "We want smart and critical readers to have a more visible role on our site" (Goldberg 2018). Readers send their letters to the editors, who then decide what gets published.

But, for those who wish to engage in real time during news events or programs, comments during livestreams offer that forum. The concept of many voices has deep roots. John Stuart Mill wrote about the importance of human expression in *On Liberty*. "If all mankind minus one, were of one opinion, mankind would be no more justified in silencing that one person, than he, if he had the power, would be justified in silencing mankind" (1863, 35).

Breaking news and citizen livestreams

> Something is wrong with our plane! It appears we are going down! Emergency landing!! Southwest flight from NYC to Dallas!!

The *Facebook Live* video shows passenger Marty Martinez in his seat wearing an oxygen mask, bumping along as Southwest Airlines Flight 1380 descends for an emergency landing (Martinez 2018). The video soon becomes a centerpiece for mainstream media coverage, grabbed and broadcast on live TV, embedded into web stories, clipped, and edited into videos, and shared on social media. Tweets shout "TERRIFYING" (*Fox 5 DC* 2018), and headlines command, "WATCH | Passenger live streams plane's descent after engine" (*Reuters and Times Live* 2018).

By the next morning, Martinez's video garners more than a half-million views on his *Facebook* account alone. Add to that the clips in news coverage online and on-air, and that scene has likely reached millions. A video search on *Facebook* for "southwest emergency landing" the next morning yielded nearly 100 news organizations, many garnering substantial numbers, such as *Fox 32 Chicago*, with nearly 1 million views (2018), and *NowThis*, with upwards of 746,000 (2018).

This is another example of how livestreams fit into the concept of *flow*. Not only do they reach us in their raw, live form, but flow onto our screens as they're integrated into mainstream news coverage, posted online, and shared on social media.

They also illustrate Zelizer's contemporary period of eyewitnessing, which, through technology and nonconventional journalists, provides a "strategically useful way to accomplish eyewitnessing, even when it has chipped away at journalism's own centrality" (2007, 425). Livestreams during emergencies, like the Marty Martinez broadcast, can offer the illusion of news media's presence on the scene "as witnesses of events they have not witnessed," which "extends journalistic authority in questionable ways" (Zelizer 2007, 425).

The practice is not limited to streams from the general public, though. Independent journalist Emily Molli says her video finds its way onto mainstream news platforms. "Now they'll take your footage or my footage and play it on their channels, and be like, 'this is footage from on the ground'" (2018). "And, they'll do it without permission as well," says independent journalist Alejandro Alvarez. Instead, they simply grant credit (2018). He sees a shortage in field reporting at news organizations, despite its importance: "There really is a lot of value in being out there, being in the field and talking to people. That seems to have been lost in the way that the media industry is progressing nowadays" (2018).

But citizen livestreams can help lead journalists to sources during breaking news, even when they're not in the field. A *CBS Evening News* livestream on *Facebook* included a phone interview with Martinez while he was still on the plane. The anchor acknowledged seeing his video, but *CBS* didn't show it. Instead, the liveshot featured the plane on the ground during the interview. In it, Martinez tells the anchorwoman that an explosion blew out a window just two rows over from him. "Was this a packed plane, was anyone sitting in row 17?" she asks. "Yeah, and that actually – hold on one second," he says. About ten seconds pass, and he comes back on the line to say he's getting off the plane. He continues talking for a few moments, and then the audio cuts out (*CBS* 2018).

Volatility during an emergency makes this type of interview compelling, but also carries risk, such as impeding events as they're unfolding on the scene. And, there's the potential an eyewitness still in the midst of a traumatic event could be in shock. Without a physical presence on the scene, journalists may miss such nuanced issues.

As livestreaming evolves as a story form, non-traditional journalists are increasingly contributing to the *flow* through social media platforms. The next chapter examines some of these livestreams in the context of social issues – from racial injustice to immigration.

References

Al Jazeera English. 2015. *Facebook*, October 9. www.facebook.com/aljazeera/phot os/a.10150243828793690.369310.7382473689/10153781845613690/

Alvarez, A. 2018. "Antifa vs. far right: Front lines of the culture war." *Subverse*, August 21. www.youtube.com/watch?time_continue=32&v=ve53EJA0kHE

Artwick, C. 2018. "Social media livestreaming." In S. Eldridge II and B. Franklin, Eds., *The Routledge Handbook of Developments in Digital Journalism Studies*. Abingdon: Routledge.

Bild. 2017. "Video diary of the Bild reporter: Live transfer of an escape from hell." *Bild*. www.bild.de/politik/ausland/zuwanderung/flucht-aus-der-hoelle-das-video-42352374.bild.html

BuzzFeed News. 2018a. "Massive crowds are once again gathering across the country: One year after the historic women's marches around the world." *Periscope Livestream*, January 20. www.pscp.tv/w/1DXGyEjgVygGM?q=buzzfeed

BuzzFeed News. 2018b. "Thousands of teachers are on strike in Oklahoma to protest low salaries and reduced spending on students." *Periscope*, April 2. www.pscp. tv/w/1yoKMkelMRXJQ

Captain, S. 2011. "Inside Occupy Wall Street's kinda: Secret media HQ." *Wired*, November 16. www.wired.com/2011/11/inside-ows-media-hq/

CBC. 2018a. "CBC News: The National was live." *Facebook Livestream*, March 5. www.facebook.com/thenational/videos/vb.62680227685/10155465008772686/? type=2&theater

CBC. 2018b. *Facebook Page, CBS News: The National*. www.facebook.com/thenational/

CBS. 2017. "Report says it's time to put the brakes on most high-speed chases." *CBS News*, July 13. www.cbsnews.com/news/high-speed-chases-risk-los-angeles-california-report/

CBS. 2018. "CBS Evening News with Jeff Glor." *Facebook Livestream*, April 17. www.facebook.com/CBSEveningNews/videos/10156467047144073/

Dredge, S. 2015. "How live video on Periscope helped 'get inside' the Syrian refugees story." *The Guardian*, September 13. www.theguardian.com/media/2015/sep/13/periscope-app-syrian-refugees-bild

Ellis, J. 2015. "What happened after 7 news sites got rid of reader comments." *NiemanLab*, September 16. www.niemanlab.org/2015/09/what-happened-after-7-news-sites-got-rid-of-reader-comments/

Fenlon, B. 2017. "Dos and don'ts for Facebook Live." *Online News Association Conference Session*, October 7. https://ona17.journalists.org/sessions/facebooklive/

Fox 32 Chicago. 2018. "TERRIFYING: Video from inside a Southwest Airlines plane shows passengers securing oxygen masks after an engine exploded." *Facebook*, April 17. www.facebook.com/Fox32Chicago/videos/10156642486747494/

Fox 5 DC. 2018. *Tweet: Fox 5 DC Twitter*, April 17. https://twitter.com/fox5dc/status/986292072809283586?ref_src=twsrc%5Etfw&ref_url=https%3A%2F%2Ftwxplorer.knightlab.com%2Fsearch%2F5ad66da6ccef1644773eeaf2%2F

Goldberg, J. 2018. "We want to hear from you: Introducing The Atlantic's new Letters section." *The Atlantic*, February 2. www.theatlantic.com/letters/archive/2018/02/we-want-to-hear-from-you/552170/

Jensen, E. 2016. "NPR website to get rid of comments." *NPR*, August 17. www.npr.org/sections/ombudsman/2016/08/17/489516952/npr-website-to-get-rid-of-comments

Jett, J. 2018. In Murphy.

Kimmel, A. 2018a. Telephone interview with author, March 9.

Kimmel, A. 2018b. *Twitter*, April 2. https://twitter.com/andrewkimmel/status/980840303593754624

Kovach, B. and Rosenstiel, T. 2010. *Blur: How to Know What's True in the Age of Information Overload*. New York: Bloomsbury USA.

Lenzner, B. 2014. "The emergence of Occupy Wall Street and digital video practices: Tim Pool, live streaming and experimentations in citizen journalism." *Studies in Documentary Film*, 83: 251–266.

Lewis, P. 2015a. "Rand Paul: The Guardian interview on Periscope." April 9. www.theguardian.com/us-news/2015/apr/09/ask-rand-paul-periscope-guardian-conversation

Lewis, P. 2015b. "The Baltimore riots: The night on Periscope: Video." *The Guardian*, April 28. www.theguardian.com/us-news/video/2015/apr/28/the-baltimore-riots-the-night-on-periscope-video

Lewis, P. 2015c. "Baltimore unrest: Periscope captures tense build-up to curfew: Video." *The Guardian*, April 29. www.theguardian.com/us-news/video/2015/apr/29/baltimore-riots-periscope-captures-tense-build-up-to-curfew-video

Lewis, P. 2018. In Artwick.

Martinez, M. 2018. "Marty Martinez was live." *Facebook Live*, April 17. www.facebook.com/marty.martinez.96/videos/10211397296550342/

Mill, J. S. 1863. *On Liberty*. Boston: Ticknor and Fields. https://books.google.com/books?id=7DcoAAAAYAAJ&printsec=frontcover&dq=on+liberty+john+stuart+mill&hl=en&sa=X&ved=0ahUKEwjZzNmEzoXZAhWltlkKHRvNDPAQ6AE IKTAA#v=onepage&q&f=false

Molli, E. 2018. "Antifa vs. far right: Front lines of the culture war." *Subverse*, August 21. www.youtube.com/watch?time_continue=32&v=ve53EJA0kHE

Mundel, S. 2017. In *CBS News*, July 13.

Mundel, S. 2018. "WATCH LIVE: Police are in a standoff with a man who claims he has bombs: @Stu_Mundel is overhead in SKY2." *Cbs Los Angeles, Periscope*, March 7. www.pscp.tv/w/1YqxoLBnqLyKv?q=cbsla

Murphy, M. 2018. "The New York Times was live." *Facebook Live*, January 21. www.facebook.com/nytimes/videos/vl.13676983433555668/10151461701314999/?type=1&theater

The New York Times. 2017. "Women's March highlights: Viewer questions." January 21. www.nytimes.com/interactive/2017/01/21/us/questions-march-live.html?_r=0

Nigro, M. 2018. In *BuzzFeed News* 2018a.

NowThis. 2018. "At least one person is dead after a Southwest Airlines flight made an emergency landing due to a failed engine." *Facebook*, April 17. www.facebook.com/NowThisNews/videos/1910654885691293/

Peters, J. 2001. "Witnessing." *Media, Culture & Society*, 236: 707–723. http://journals.sagepub.com/doi/10.1177/016344301023006002

Reuters and *Times Live*. 2018. "WATCH | Passenger live streams plane's descent after engine explodes midair." *Times Live*, April 18. www.timeslive.co.za/news/world/2018-04-18-watch-passenger-live-streams-planes-descent-after-engine-explodes-midair/

Rodriguez, G. 2017. "Gloria Rodriguez WTVD was live." *Facebook Live*, August 16. www.facebook.com/GloriaRodriguezWTVD/videos/1741619422544766/

Rodriguez, R. 2015. "Periscope: Four ways it's shaking up media." *CNN*, 26 May. www.cnn.com/2015/05/26/tech/periscope-android-media/

Simon, S. 2018. "This week's essay on the other man in a photo that went viral: An act of kindness captured." *Periscope*, March 17. www.pscp.tv/nprscottsimon/1DXGyXZDmDEKM

Sorge, L. 2018. In *BuzzFeed News* 2018a.

Thomaidis, I. 2017. "Dos and don'ts for Facebook Live." *Online News Association Conference Session*, October 7. https://ona17.journalists.org/sessions/facebooklive/

Wang, F. 2018. "#Sacramento protestors shutting down the freeway for #StephonClark." *Periscope*, March 22. www.pscp.tv/FrancesWangTV/1MYxNpEzwqbGw

WILX. 2018a. "WILX News 10 was live." *Facebook Live*, March 2. www.facebook.com/wilxnews10/videos/1716013631775439/

WILX. 2018b. "WILX News 10 was live." *Facebook Live*, March 2. www.facebook.com/wilxnews10/videos/1715798575130278/

Witty, P. 2015. *Twitter*, September 26. https://twitter.com/patrickwitty/status/647842356922871808

Zelizer, B. 2007. "On 'having been there': 'Eyewitnessing' as a journalistic key word." *Critical Studies in Media Communication*, 245: 408–428. www.tandfonline.com/doi/abs/10.1080/07393180701694614

3 Citizen livestreams – a force for good?

It's Super Bowl Sunday and protesters are blocking the Metro tracks near U.S. Bank Stadium in downtown Minneapolis. Bright yellow text emblazoned on their black shirts shouts,

YOU CAN'T PLAY WITH BLACK LIVES.

Fists raised, they're chant-singing,

> *Ancestors watching, I know, I know.*
> *Ancestors watching, I know, I know.*

Racial injustice and livestreaming

More than 4,000 virtual bystanders watch live on *Periscope* as Black Visions Collective streams the scene unfolding on the tracks (2018). A woman on a bullhorn shouts,

> *You colonized our homes.* The crowd responds,
> *We always resisted.*
>
> *You put us in chains.*
> *We always resisted.*
>
> *You exploited our labor.*
> *We always resisted.*
>
> *You took Jamar, Philando, and Marcus from us.*
> *We always resisted.*

These men had been victims of police shootings. And now, amidst the excitement of game day, reminders of police brutality and racial tensions share the spotlight. One of the men they named – Philando Castile – had received global attention after his girlfriend, Diamond Reynolds, streamed his death on *Facebook Live*. A police officer shot him during a traffic stop near Minneapolis in 2016.

"Oh my God, please don't tell me he's dead," Reynolds pleads, the camera revealing a bleeding, writhing Castile. With her boyfriend dying beside her and four-year-old daughter in the back seat, Reynolds continues to broadcast – into the police car and while handcuffed. As she sobs, her child comforts her, "It's OK. I'm right here with you" (*MPR News* 2016).

The shooting and Reynolds' live video quickly became a top news story, with more than 3 million views on *Facebook* and "countless millions" on television by noon the next day (Stelter 2016). It stands out among citizen livestreams for its emotion and raw, graphic scene, but also for its place in the larger context of violence and race. And, it's recognized as precedence-setting in social media livestreaming for its ability to galvanize (Benson-Allott 2016). Nearly 40 peaceful demonstrations followed, *The Washington Post* reported, "during which protesters marched and demanded consequences" (Saslow 2016).

And there was violence. The night after Castile died, a sniper opened fire during a protest in Dallas (Kenning 2018). Michael KB Mason livestreamed on the scene (2016). As sirens scream, we see a close-up of his face as he's walking. "Holy sh*t," he exclaims. Then, more sirens, and again, "Holy sh*t." As he switches the view to the street, we see at least three police cruisers, and hear what sounds like shots firing (Mason 2016). The sniper kills five police officers – an apparent retribution for police brutality against black people (Kenning 2018).

The attack in Dallas came on the heels of not only Castile's death, but another fatal shooting of an African American male. Just one day earlier, police in Baton Rouge, Louisiana, had shot and killed Alton Sterling (Fausset 2018). NFL quarterback Colin Kaepernick tweeted his outrage over the two killings and linked to the video of Castile dying. "We are under attack! It's clear as day! Less than 24 hrs later another body in the street!" (2016).

Demonstrations continued into the weekend. In Baton Rouge, DeRay McKesson opened up his *Periscope* app to broadcast as he walked with protesters (2016). Flashing blue lights illuminate the street as squad cars creep by. The crowd shouts, "No justice, no peace. No racist police." McKesson narrates as the scene unfolds. "Protesters haven't hurt anybody, weren't blocking the street or anything. And the police are just snatching and grabbing people." The chants continue, and McKesson's narration goes on, "The police in Baton Rouge have been truly awful tonight. They provoked people. They chased people just for kicks. . . . The police have been violent tonight, the protesters have not."

Car horns blare as the chants continue, "No justice, no peace. No racist police." A man's voice off camera warns, "If I see you in the road and I get close to you, you're going to jail." McKesson says, "I think he's talking to me y'all." Viewers respond, "Stay Safe," and "Please comply!!!!!!!! Just do what they're saying."

"Watch the police, they are literally just provoking people," says McKesson. Then, from behind, a man yells, "Police! You're under arrest!" The camera goes every which way. "Wha. . . !! I'm under arrest y'all," McKesson cries, and apparently drops the phone. Bystanders shout to police, "Why is he being arrested? He didn't do anything!" McKesson's livestream continues, but now a woman narrates. We hear crying behind her. "It's OK, he's gonna be OK, babe. I know." As she walks, she says, "They took him away in an armored vehicle." She asks viewers to call the Baton Rouge police to demand he be released. Fighting back tears, she says, "If you pray, I need you to pray. Because we know what they do to us in jail cells."

Nearly 700,000 people have watched the *Periscope* video. McKesson was released after spending 16 hours in a Baton Rouge jail cell (Alcindor 2016).

Soon after the killings and protests, Kaepernick sits on the bench during the national anthem in silent protest of violence against African-Americans at the hands of police (Branch 2017). He later kneels, and others follow in the #TakeAKnee protest.

"I am not going to stand up to show pride in a flag for a country that oppresses black people and people of color," Kaepernick told *NFL Media*. "To me, this is bigger than football and it would be selfish on my part to look the other way. There are bodies in the street and people getting paid leave and getting away with murder" (Wyche 2016).

Jeronimo Yanez, the police officer who shot Castile, had been placed on paid administrative leave. The following June, a jury found him not guilty in the fatal shooting of Philando Castile (Xiong 2017). Protests again broke out. And as demonstrators marched through St. Paul and onto Interstate 94, shutting it down, participants and news media streamed live on social media. Volunteer media collective *Unicorn Riot* was on the highway as demonstrators faced off against police (2017). "You have five minutes to disperse," a state trooper announced on a bullhorn.

Some leave, while others chant, clap hands, and hold their ground. "Black lives, they matter here. Black lives, they matter here." The male reporter wearing a helmet, with a gas mask around his neck, narrates as the camera follows him through the crowd. A woman on a bullhorn shouts, "Philando." The crowd responds, "Castile." They go on for minutes, holding a banner, "He was someone's son." Men have taken off their shirts, wrapping them around their faces as masks, ready for tear gas. Police use a sound cannon, warning arrests are coming. Later, as police move in and make arrests, demonstrators chant, "The world is watching, the world is watching."

Livestreams serve as real-time social witnessing. "Being an eyewitness is hard," says human rights advocate Yvette Alberdingk Thijm in a Ted Talk on truth and justice (2017). "Your story will get denied. Your video will get lost in a sea of images. Your story will not be trusted. And you will be targeted." But, she argues, livestream witnessing can make a difference. "Now the tables are turned. The distant witnesses, the watching audience, they matter" (Thijm 2017).

Again, nearly two years after the Philando Castile shooting, hundreds of thousands watch and witness anew, as protests erupt following another shooting of a black man. The family grieves for Stephon Clark, killed by Sacramento Police in his grandmother's backyard. He was unarmed.

Vigils and marches follow, for days and nights, livestreamed by demonstrators, bystanders, and reporters. Protesters block the entrance to a King's game at Golden 1 Center in downtown Sacramento, "Black lives," (crowd responds) "Matter!" Then, in unison, "Black lives matter, black lives matter, black lives matter!" (Light 2018).

They march onto a freeway, chanting:

> *Shut! – It! – Down!*
> *Shut! – It! – Down!*
> *Shut – It – Down! Shut! – It! – Down! Shut! – It! – Down!*
>
> (Wang 2018)

Nearly 100,000 people watch them demonstrate at City Hall.

> *What do we do?*
> *Stand up, fight back!*
>
> *What do we do?*
> *Stand up, fight back!*
>
> *What do we do?*
> *Stand up, fight back!*
>
> (Kempa 2018)

A private autopsy finds that eight bullets hit Clark – none from the front. "This independent autopsy affirms that Stephon was not a threat to police and was slain in another senseless police killing under increasingly questionable circumstances," said Benjamin Crump, the family's lawyer, as reported in *The New York Times* (Robles and Del Real 2018).

That night, a protest becomes volatile. As people lock arms, forming a line to block the freeway, the livestreamer moves through the crowd, narrating – but the shouts drown him out. "Get that f*in' camera out of his face! I'll slap that sh*t out your f*in' hand" (*CCC Advocate* 2018).

The livestreamer appears on camera and provides context, "Protesters have repeatedly knocked cameras out of hands, they've tried to get people from being in front." Later, he shows a black man standing in front of a cop who is wearing a face-shield helmet. The protester holds up his phone to the cop and says, "Guess what, it's a cell phone not a gun" (*CCC Advocate* 2018).

Independent journalist Alejandro Alvarez has seen protesters restricting media access at other events. "Everybody is always trying to maintain control of the narrative," he said. "That's something that we're seeing happen a lot these days. That's why people seem to rely on having activists do their own media" (Alvarez 2018).

Across the country in New York City, demonstrators confront police at a solidarity march. Livestreams again allow viewers worldwide to bear witness (Kris10 2018; *BuzzFeed News* 2018).

And, soon after, in Brooklyn, "Police shot another innocent dude right on my block," says a man's voice as he narrates the scene in the street live on *Periscope*. "This is just like a hour ago" (ziggy 2018). New York City police shot and killed Saheed Vassell as he pointed a metal pipe at them that looked like a gun (Mueller and Schweber 2018).

The Washington Post has been tracking fatal shootings by U.S. police since 2015, the year after police in Ferguson, Missouri, killed unarmed black teenager Michael Brown. Killings of unarmed people dropped dramatically in the first year – by almost half. And, so far, they appear lower in 2018 (Sullivan, Tate, and Jenkins 2018). Experts say it's too early to draw solid conclusions from these data, but suggest that the use of video "provided a visual record of events that otherwise might have been described only by the officers involved" (Sullivan, Tate, and Jenkins 2018).

This would include police body cam and helicopter video, eyewitness cell phone video, and livestreams. The camera phone has given citizens "a powerful means for bearing witness to brutality" (Anden-Papadopoulos 2013, 760).

Witnessing through livestream in real time opens a window to the actual event. As John Durham Peters wrote in his seminal work on witnessing, "Liveness serves as an assurance of access to truth and authenticity" (2001, 719). Today, a distant witness can interact with the livestreamer and people on the scene, as well as with others who are watching in real time. This connection, even in the absence of physical presence, offers a level of witnessing that goes beyond virtual viewing.

In addition, livestream as *flow* (discussed in Chapter 1) appears to be playing a role in public exposure to these shootings and subsequent outrage and scrutiny. Not only do we partake of these broadcasts in real time, but salient moments make their way to our screens via video clips, still frames, and journalists' storytelling. And our social networks bring the added dimension of commenting and discussion.

White supremacy and livestreaming as propaganda

Men clad in cream-colored shirts and khaki pants carry torches as they walk up Charlottesville's Market Street, to a statue, draped in a tarp.

A single voice shouts, "You will not replace us," starting a chant that the crowd repeats 15 times. Richard Spencer is livestreaming on *Periscope*, as he and his followers return to the city where they marched two months earlier and clashed with counter protesters (Spencer 2017a). And where a Dodge Challenger roared through a crowd of pedestrians, killing Heather Heyer. They sing, "I wish I was in Dixie, Hooray! Hooray! In Dixieland I'll take my stand to live and die in Dixie." And before they hustle away and Spencer ends the stream, they again shout, "You will not replace us. You will not replace us" (Spencer 2017a).

Viewership is high for Spencer's October torch march livestream – nearly 100,000 watched on *Periscope*. According to the Anti-Defamation League, white supremacist propaganda on college campuses more than tripled in 2017 (ADL 2018).

> These campaigns are designed to spread the white supremacist message, recruit followers, and garner attention. Many of the groups (particularly IE, Patriot Front, and Vanguard America) also photograph or livestream their campus activism for use in online propaganda.
>
> (ADL 2018)

The live videos are rich in symbols – both visual and verbal. At the heart of propaganda is "the control of attitudes by the manipulation of symbols" (Lasswell and Blumenstock 1939, 9).

Later that month, Spencer livestreams in Gainesville, Florida. Despite public opposition to his appearance there, his own *Periscope* livestreams have garnered thousands of views. As he takes the stage, the crowd erupts, "Fu*k you, Spencer! Fu*k you, Spencer!" He asks people to raise their hand if they identify with the alt-right. The crowd boos. About 15 minutes in, they chant "Go home, Spencer! Go home, Spencer! Go home, Spencer!" (2017b).

The tension is high – another factor in fueling propaganda. "The propagandist who deals with a community when its tension level is high, finds that a reservoir of explosive energy can be touched off by the same small match which would normally ignite a bonfire" (Lasswell 1938, 190).

The livestream provides a venue to fuel the fire. Comments posted to *Periscope* are largely from Spencer supporters: @NorthernBreeze7 "We cannot be stopped," @paulyg1 "Hail Spencer," @MurdochMan "Hose them down lol," @daytripper 55 "White lives matter," @daviddwatsonn "I love you Spenser," and @kitover "Not going home! We're never going it's too late" (Spencer 2017b).

His cameraman shows the crowd and says, "They are doing Black Power salutes to us."

Outside the arena, another visual symbol agitates the crowd – the swastika. A man wearing a T-shirt emblazoned with swastikas is surrounded by angry faces. They shout, "Fu*k off, Nazi puss" (*BuzzFeed News* 2017). Tension escalates as protesters spit at, shove, punch, and grab him. Cell phones encircle him, held high. A black man wearing dreadlocks and a jean jacket gets inches from his face and shouts, "Why the fu*k you don't like me?" and then grabs him in a big bear hug. Other protesters shout, "Get him out of here!" and "Nazi, go! Nazi, go!" (*BuzzFeed News* 2017).

Later, as the protest is breaking up, a silver jeep pulls up to a group of protesters waiting at a bus stop (Svrluga and Rozsa 2017). The men, whom police identified as white nationalists, "threatened the group, making Nazi salutes and shouting chants about Hitler," police said. Then, one of the men fired a shot at the protesters (Svrluga and Rozsa 2017). According to *The Guardian*, police arrested three men in relation to the incident. Tyler Tenbrink admitted he was the shooter (Beckett 2017).

In an interview with *The Gainesville Sun* during the protest, Tenbrink said he had driven to Gainesville from Houston to see Spencer speak.

"This is a mess. I'm disappointed in the course of things," he said. "It appears that the only answer left is violence, and nobody wants that" (Strange 2017).

Charlottesville attack

Violence has been on the rise in the alt-right movement, with 17 killed and 43 injured in 2017 – the most violent year as reported by the Southern Poverty Law Center (Hankes and Amend 2018). Perpetrators shot, stabbed, and drove down their victims, in some cases on video and in livestreams. The "Unite the Right" rally in Charlottesville, Virginia, was no exception.

In the oppressive August heat, Faith Goldy walks with a crowd in downtown Charlottesville, broadcasting on *Periscope*. A woman behind her wearing a Black Lives Matter T-shirt shouts, "Are you from the alt-right? Get away from here. Get away from here" (Goldy 2017a). Goldy smiles and responds, "I'm looking to learn about inclusion, guys." She then reaches for the camera to change the view toward the marchers, and says, "All right, here you go." Within five seconds, a greenish-grey car speeds through the crowd, and she shrieks, "Oh, sh*t. Oh, sh*t. Holy sh*t. Holy sh*t. Holy sh*t. Oh God. Oh God. Oh God." The camera shot gets bumpy as she moves away, saying, "I'm going to a safe space, guys." She then turns the lens toward herself, wearing a look of disbelief. "Saw *(garbled)*, just ran over a whole bunch of protesters." She covers her mouth and shakes her head. "A lot of people got hit." Andrew Marantz wrote in *The New Yorker* that Goldy's *Periscope* was "The most arresting video I saw this year" (2017a).

At the same time, Ford Fischer was broadcasting on *Facebook Live* from the periphery of the march when people approach screaming, "Run! Run!" (2017). A woman in a pink bandanna yells, "Ambulance, call an ambulance," and he asks, "What happened?" She points toward the crowd. "A car just drove straight in." She shouts back toward the scene, "You motherf*er." Fischer walks into the crowd and goes on camera briefly, saying it's chaos. He approaches people on the ground. You can see a leg and shoe. A woman shields the area, arms outstretched to block the view. A man's voice screams, "Sidewalk! Everybody on the f*ing sidewalk, now!"

Fischer turns the camera toward himself, wet hair escaping his helmet. "Several people have been seriously injured," he says. He appears to be holding back tears. "They're performing CPR in front of me. It doesn't look good at all. Viewer discretion is advised." Police clear back the crowd as an ambulance arrives. They carry away a victim on a stretcher. Viewers express horror as Fischer zooms in on blood in the street, posting "Omg," and "Oh my lord!" (Fischer 2017). The attack killed 32-year-old Heather Heyer and injured dozens more (Wilson 2017).

Neither Fischer nor Goldy were mainstream media journalists at the time. He was there as an independent videographer, and for his company *News-2Share*. Goldy was with Canadian conservative media, *TheRebel*. She was let go shortly after, for going on the *Daily Stormer* podcast, said Ezra Levant of *TheRebel* (2017). The *Daily Stormer* is a neo-Nazi website run by alt-right neo-Nazi extremist Andrew Anglin (SPLC undated).

Goldy said many haters "wished me dead" after her livestream (2017b). Her reporting on anti-fascist groups, or "antifa," was "representative of a theme that had risen from far-right media to the mainstream since President Trump's inauguration," wrote Dave Weigel in *The Washington Post* (2017). That theme has been presented as "a rising danger to law and order, a justification for alt-right organizations to organize armed rallies – and for ordinary Americans to arm themselves, too" (Weigel 2017). Goldy later carried that theme to Canada. Nearly 50,000 watched her *Periscope*

"ANTIFA BLOCKADE AT BORDER RALLY" (2018). Her Charlottesville livestream was "transformed into police evidence," wrote Weigel (2017).

After the violence, public figures in Virginia also broadcast live. At Heather Heyer's funeral, the state's governor, Terry McAuliffe, streams on *Periscope*. "No parent should ever have to go through losing a child," he says to a group gathered around him as "Amazing Grace" plays in the distance (2017). And in a gesture toward healing, musician Dave Matthews organizes *A Concert for Charlottesville*, which is livestreamed. Ariana Grande, Pharrell Williams, Justin Timberlake, and Stevie Wonder showcase the event (Hamilton 2017).

But in the days following the attack, contention raged on social media and in the mainstream news while the statue behind the controversy remained standing in Charlottesville's Emancipation Park. Elsewhere, Confederate monuments would soon come down. Protesters in Durham, North Carolina, toppled a statue of a Confederate soldier, which was recorded, shared, and viewed by millions (Barajas 2017). And in Baltimore, a crew dismantled its Confederate monuments under the cover of darkness, to intercept violence (Campbell and Broadwater 2017).

Ten days after the killing, Charlottesville wraps the Lee statue in a black tarp (Held 2018). *WMC* news livestreams on *Facebook*, polling on screen as the scene unfolds, "Do you support covering Confederate statues?" asks the "LiveU" poll (2017).

Months pass, and the statue of Robert E. Lee stands unshrouded in Emancipation Park, on display once again after a judge orders the tarps be removed. White nationalists continue their demonstrations, marching in Georgia and burning a giant swastika while giving the Nazi salute and shouting, "Sieg Heil" (Gray 2018), hail to victory (Collins 2010). Videos and still images showcase these symbols, and appear in mainstream news and social networks.

At about the same time, *Facebook*'s Mark Zuckerberg testifies before U.S. Congress, stating "We do not allow hate groups on Facebook overall. If there's a group that, their primary purpose or a large part of what they do is spreading hate, we will ban them from the platform overall" (Zuckerberg 2018). Within days, *Facebook* shuts down Richard Spencer's accounts (Dalrymple II 2018). And, after being briefly locked on *Twitter*, Spencer tweeted, "I'm under attack. And I need your help" (Spencer 2018).

The link goes to a page on Funded Justice.

> Some of the biggest, baddest law firms in the country are suing me, along with other prominent figures. . . . They are going after those who organized – or, in my case, attended – the Unite The Right rally on August 12 in Charlottesville, Virginia.
>
> (2018)

As of this writing, his *Periscope* account remains open; however, searching for "Richard Spencer" in the app does not produce his account in the results. *Twitter* asserts it is not shadow banning, that is, "deliberately making someone's content undiscoverable" (Gadde and Beykpour 2018). But it does rank tweets and search results, to address what it calls "bad-faith actors who intend to manipulate or detract from healthy conversation" (Gadde and Beykpour 2018).

Immigration, Muslims, and terrorism

Revelers in the Village step, Samba, and shimmy through the New York City neighborhood on Halloween. "There's a lot of Wonder Woman here," observes Jamie Stelter as she co-anchors parade coverage, livestreamed on Spectrum News NY1. "Tonight is all about resilience after what we saw today" (Stelter 2017). Just a few hours earlier, a terrorist killed eight people as he rammed a truck onto a bike path less than a mile away. Near the crime scene, just down the street from the parade, a woman narrates a stream on *Periscope*. In contrast to Stelter's positive focus and the parade's festive unity, the tone of the *Periscope* stream is caustic and divisive.

As the streamer nears the World Trade Center she says, "They love reminding us of 9/11. They're sick. They're sick, demented people. That's what Islam is. OK, and if you're offended – too f*ing bad" (she says the expletive). She continues walking toward flashing red lights.

"It's so upsetting to see things like this. In America. And people want to criticize Donald Trump for running a Muslim ban, but this is what you get when you import masses of uncivilized savages." Viewers send a spray of hearts up the screen. This is only the beginning of nearly three hours of Laura Loomer's livestream, watched by nearly 35,000 viewers (Loomer 2017a).

As the stream unfolds, she confronts a woman in a hijab, "Excuse me, I really would like to know, you know, you're coming out here dressed in full Muslim garb, at the scene of like a terrorist attack, do you disavow this attack that just took place?" A male voice exclaims, "That's so rude." Loomer shouts back, "I don't care if it's rude" (Loomer 2017a).

Another woman says to Loomer, "You are so ignorant." They argue and shout, while viewers send hearts, which flow up the side of the screen. Later in the stream Loomer spots CNN's Anderson Cooper and heckles him during his broadcast from the street. "You guys are Fake News, Anderson. Fake News. Fake news Anderson Cooper." She continues, "Why aren't they talking about the fact that this guy was an Islamic immigrant?" (Loomer 2017a).

The stream cuts off and she starts again. Other passersby confront her: "It's racist to say that. It's absolutely racist to say that. You shouldn't be saying that." She responds, "I'm gonna say it, I don't care" (2017b). After much shouting the stream cuts off.

At some points, the livestreams with their histrionics seem to take on the essence of staged reality TV. Like a few months earlier, when Loomer stormed the performance of Julius Caesar in Central Park and streamed it on *Periscope* (2017c). "Shame on all of you. Shame! Shame on all of you for promoting political violence against Donald Trump," she shouts. "Stop the normalization of political violence against the right" (Loomer 2017c).

In another stream, in handcuffs, Loomer tells her viewers,

> I'm just trying to protect Donald Trump. I'm trying to protect the right, because we're under attack. These people want to kill us. They're stabbing someone that looks exactly like Donald Trump inside that theater. And they're trying to kill us. And I'm not going to let that happen.
>
> (2017d)

Who is Laura Loomer? Her *Facebook* page says she's an "investigative journalist" (2018a). *RebelMedia* has a *YouTube* page for her that calls her a "right-wing investigative journalist and activist" (2018).

Others have referred to her as a "far-right activist" (Jeltsen 2018), "right-wing activist" (Marantz 2017b), and "professional troll" (Weill and LaPorta 2018). In today's attention economy, where "attention has become a more valuable currency than the kind you store in bank accounts" (Davenport and Beck 2001), Loomer and her streams have *not* gone unnoticed. She's got 243,000 followers on *Twitter*, and views on *Periscope* often top 100,000, such as her stage-storming in Central Park and at James Comey's book tour (Loomer 2018b). The night Loomer heckled Anderson Cooper, right-wing provocateur Mike Cernovich tweeted, "Anderson Cooper shut down the CNN news cast after being heckled by onlookers. Now they know how it feels when we want to give a talk" (2017). Cooper quipped, "Actually my broadcast ends at 10 p.m. . . . every night . . . like clockwork" (2017).

Others are less tolerant. Loomer's tweet about Muslim Uber and Lyft drivers got her banned from the ride-sharing services (Reuters 2017).

> I'm late to the NYPD press conference because I couldn't find a non Muslim cab or @Uber @lyft driver for over 30 min! This is insanity.
>
> 11:40 AM – 1 Nov 2017 from Manhattan,
> NY (author's screen shot)

The tweet no longer exists on her *Twitter* account. But, as of this writing, her *Periscope* and *Twitter* accounts are active. However, Loomer did lose her blue "Verified" checkmark after the Muslim driver tweet.

Twitter notes the reasons for removing user verification, including: "Promoting hate and/or violence against, or directly attacking or threatening other people on the basis of race, ethnicity, national origin, sexual orientation, gender, gender identity, religious affiliation, age, disability, or disease," and "Inciting or engaging in harassment of others" (*Twitter* Help Center 2018).

Periscope guidelines state, "Do not engage in dialogue or behavior that: Intends only to incite or engage in the targeted harassment of others. This includes content that promotes the abuse of other people or the disruption of another person's broadcasting experience" (2018).

In her *Twitter* bio, Loomer frames losing her verification as: "UnVerified for speaking truth" (2018c). However, others may interpret her language and actions as violating those terms of service.

In mid-May 2018, Loomer traveled to Israel for the U.S. embassy opening in Jerusalem and appeared live on Alex Jones' *InfoWars* during that visit. Since then, *YouTube* and *Facebook* have removed much of Jones' content from their sites, noting violations of their policies regarding hate speech and glorifying violence (Nicas 2018). His live interview with Loomer appears to have been included in that removal (*InfoWars* 2018).[1] Note, however, that his *Twitter* and *Periscope* accounts remained intact until September 6, 2018, when Twitter shut them down (Twitter Safety 2018).

During Loomer's visit to Jerusalem, Israeli troops killed 60 and injured thousands of Palestinians protesting at the Israeli border in Gaza, just 40 miles away (*BBC* 2018). Humanitarian agencies condemned the action as "unacceptable and inhuman" (Doctors Without Borders 2018), and a "violation of international standards" (Amnesty International 2018).

Loomer tweeted, "It's too bad the United States doesn't protect its border the same way Israel does . . . #Gaza" (2018d).

Back in the states, the man Loomer once rushed the stage and risked arrest for had his own words for people who attempt to cross borders. He spoke them during a livestreamed roundtable on U.S. sanctuary cities. Major news networks, the White House, and others were broadcasting live on *Facebook*, *Periscope*, and *YouTube*, when Donald Trump said, "We have people coming into the country, or trying to come in – and we're stopping a lot of them – but we're taking people out of the country. You wouldn't believe how bad these people are. These aren't people. These are animals" (*CNN* 2018).

Viewers reacted to his comment in real time on the feeds. Many posting to *CNN*'s *Facebook* livestream were appalled:

Linda: *He just called people "animals" is this the president of a humane nation??*
Rita: *Animals????? Bad talk by this man.*
Veronica: *"These aren't people these are animals"?? Wow!!*

Rebecca: *Did he just call people animals??*

Renee: *Animals?! None of the people that I have seen ICE round up were NOT animals. They had jobs, paid taxes or were brought here as kids.*

Kelli: *were my ancestors that came over in the 1600's animals too? oh wait, i guess if they came from Europe, it's a different story*

Debra: *But ICE is rounding up hard working people with families because they got a parking ticket. Those people are not animals.*

(*CNN* 2018)

On the White House feed, responses were mixed (2018):

Nancy: *You're right Mr. President they're not people though Animals I agree with you*

Seann: *Send the animals home !!!!!! MAGA !!!*

Renee: *Oh you mean like the man who was married, with two kids and a great job. You sent him back to Ghana.*

Monica: *THANK YOU MR PRESIDENT !! REMOVE THE ANIMALS LEGAL OR ILLEGAL !!*

Jeff: *It's so much easier to scare people than inspire them. Everything is "a disgrace," everything in the past was "the worst," "the dumbest." I want to protect the country, and there are many ways to do it without becoming a police state*

On the *Fox News Facebook Live* feed, there was little response, albeit supportive of Trump (2018).

Russ: *Illegal criminals are animals. Look at the crimes they commit!*

Trump's livestreamed words made their way onto social media and in mainstream news reports, drawing outrage and criticism. Senator Diane Feinstein tweeted, "Immigrants are not 'animals.' The president's statement was deeply offensive and racist" (2018).

Trump lashed out, saying,

Fake News Media had me calling Immigrants, or Illegal Immigrants, 'Animals.' Wrong! They were begrudgingly forced to withdraw their stories. I referred to MS 13 Gang Members as 'Animals,' a big difference – and so true. Fake News got it purposely wrong, as usual!

(2018a)

Citizens can see the event in its entirety, for full context, by watching the livestreamed recording archived on social networking platforms. They can hear the actual words as they were spoken, to make their own judgment. And, they can see the conversation in comments responding to the event as it unfolds in real time.

Research shows that dehumanizing language can lead to negative attitudes toward immigrants. An experiment with non-Hispanic U.S. adults found that portraying immigrants as a "virus" or "disease" led to "more negative attitudes toward immigrants and more restrictive policy preferences" (Utych 2018, 448). The results align with previous research that found relationships between "animalistic dehumanization" and harsh judgments of out-groups (Haslam 2006).

Shortly after Trump's "animals" comment, he used another such reference in a tweet, pointing the finger at Democrats. "They don't care about crime and want illegal immigrants, no matter how bad they may be, to pour into and *infest* our Country, like MS-13" (2018b). *Infest* – a dehumanizing term relating to insects – came amidst protests against the Trump administration's immigration policy that separated thousands of migrant children from their families. U.S. elected officials adopted social media livestreaming as part of their role in addressing the humanitarian crises, as the following chapter explores.

Note

1 Alex Jones' *YouTube* account, with more than 2 million subscribers and billions of views, was removed on August 6, 2018 (Nicas 2018).

Loomer responded in a tweet: "@RealAlexJones always believed in me. He gave me a voice when others wouldn't . . . It's disgraceful what BIG TECH is doing to him & his supporters" (Loomer 2018e).

On August 7, 2018, the author attempted to access Jones' interview with Laura Loomer on the *InfoWars* website, but clicking "play" on the embedded *YouTube* video led to the message, "This video is unavailable," apparently removed along with his other *YouTube* content.

References

ADL. 2018. "White supremacist propaganda surges on campus." *Anti-Defamation League Website, ADL.org*, January 29. www.adl.org/education/resources/reports/white-supremacist-propaganda-surges-on-campus?ncid=APPLENEWS00001

Alcindor, Y. 2016. "DeRay Mckesson, arrested while protesting in Baton Rouge, is released." *The New York Times*, July 10. www.nytimes.com/2016/07/11/us/deray-mckesson-arrested-in-baton-rouge-protest.html

Alvarez, A. 2018. "Antifa vs. far right: Front lines of the culture war." *Subverse*, August 21. www.youtube.com/watch?time_continue=32&v=ve53EJA0kHE

Amnesty International. 2018. "Israel/OPT: Use of excessive force in Gaza an abhorrent violation of international law." May 14. www.amnesty.org/en/latest/news/2018/05/israelopt-use-of-excessive-force-in-gaza-an-abhorrent-violation-of-international-law/

Anden-Papadopoulos, K. 2013. "Citizen camera-witnessing: Embodied political dissent in the age of 'mediated mass self-communication'." *New Media & Society*, 165: 753–769. http://journals.sagepub.com/doi/abs/10.1177/1461444813489863?journalCode=nmsa

Barajas, J. 2017. "WATCH: Protesters pull down Confederate statue in North Carolina." *PBS News Hour*, August 14. www.pbs.org/newshour/nation/watch-protesters-pull-confederate-statue-north-carolina

BBC. 2018. "Did Israel use excessive force at Gaza protests?" *BBC News*, May 17. www.bbc.com/news/world-middle-east-44124556

Beckett, L. 2017. "Three men charged after protesters shot at following Richard Spencer speech." *The Guardian*, October 20. www.theguardian.com/us-news/2017/oct/20/gainesville-shooting-three-men-charged-florida-richard-spencer

Benson-Allott, C. 2016. "Learning from Horror." *Film Quarterly*, 70(2). http://fq.ucpress.edu/content/70/2/58

Black Visions Collective. 2018. "We have shutdown the light rail in Minneapolis #." *Periscope*, February 4. www.pscp.tv/1lPKqnEZldwGb?q=%40blacklivesmpls

Branch, J. 2017. "The awakening of Colin Kaepernick." *The New York Times*, September 7. www.nytimes.com/2017/09/07/sports/colin-kaepernick-nfl-protests.html

BuzzFeed News. 2017. "White supremacist Richard Spencer is scheduled to speak at @UF as Florida braces for possible violent protests." *Periscope*, October 19. www.pscp.tv/w/1ZkKzddDRyewJv?q=buzzfeed+news

BuzzFeed News. 2018. "Rally for Stephon Clark." *Periscope*, March.

Campbell, C. and Broadwater, L. 2017. "Citing 'safety and security,' Pugh has Baltimore Confederate monuments taken down." *The Baltimore Sun*, August 16. www.baltimoresun.com/news/maryland/baltimore-city/bs-md-ci-monuments-removed-20170816-story.html

CCC Advocate. 2018. "#StephonClark #protest in #Sacramento continues as the crowd marches in #Downtown." *Periscope*, March 30. www.pscp.tv/AccentAdvocate/1MYGNpYqQVbxw

Cernovich, M. 2017. *Twitter*, October 31. https://twitter.com/cernovich/status/925543628239380480

CNN. 2018. "CNN was live at the White House." *Facebook Live*, May 16. www.facebook.com/cnn/videos/10158348390036509/

Collins. 2010. *Collins English Dictionary Website*. www.collinsdictionary.com/us/dictionary/english/sieg-heil

Cooper, A. 2017. *Twitter*, October 31. https://twitter.com/andersoncooper/status/925546861313785857?lang=en

Dalrymple II, J. 2018. "Facebook said hate groups aren't allowed on the site: Now it has shut down white nationalist Richard Spencer's accounts." *BuzzFeed News*, April 13. www.buzzfeed.com/jimdalrympleii/facebook-just-shut-down-white-nationalist-richard-spencers?utm_term=.ukL3EXp2no#.lhJowl2GMr

Davenport, T. and Beck, J. 2001. *The Attention Economy: Understanding the New Currency of Business.* Boston: Harvard Business School Press. https://books.google.com/books/about/The_Attention_Economy.html?id=FuuKd3on9psC&printsec=frontcover&source=kp_read_button#v=onepage&q&f=false

Doctors Without Borders. 2018. "'Unacceptable and inhuman' violence by Israeli army against Palestinian protesters in Gaza." May 24. www.doctorswithoutborders.org/article/%E2%80%9Cunacceptable-and-inhuman%E2%80%9D-violence-israeli-army-against-palestinian-protesters-gaza

Fausset, R. 2018. "Baton Rouge officer is fired in Alton Sterling case as police release new videos." *The New York Times*, March 30. www.nytimes.com/2018/03/30/us/baton-rouge-alton-sterling.html

Feinstein, D. 2018. *Twitter*, May 16. https://twitter.com/SenFeinstein/status/996913253245706240

Fischer, F. 2017. "News2Share was live: At Charlottesville DowntownMall." *Facebook Live*, August 12. www.facebook.com/N2Sreports/videos/1490419907732560/

Fox News. 2018. "Fox News was live." *Facebook Live*, May 16. www.facebook.com/FoxNews/videos/10156969668776336/

Funded Justice. 2018. "Richard Spencer's legal defense fund." *Funded Justice Website*. www.fundedjustice.com/Spencer-legal?ref=tw_87FGG2_ab_5nfgeuUW9Rv5nfgeuUW9Rv

Gadde, V. and Beykpour, K. 2018. "Setting the record straight on shadow banning." *Twitter Blog*, July 26. https://blog.twitter.com/official/en_us/topics/company/2018/Setting-the-record-straight-on-shadow-banning.html

Goldy, F. 2017a. "Car crashes into crowd of protesters after rallies turned violent in Charlottesville." *Storyful, from Periscope*. www.aol.com/video/partner/storyful/517837123/598f691044a64b7fb9f32427/

Goldy, F. 2017b. "Faith Goldy: Charlottesville, in my own words." *Rebel Media YouTube Video*, August 14. www.youtube.com/watch?v=u8WPz2u1ipA

Goldy, F. 2018. "Antifa blockade at border rally." *Periscope*, June. www.pscp.tv/w/1djGXdVLvVXGZ?q=faith+goldy

Gray, S. 2018. "Neo-Nazis burned a Swastika after their rally in Georgia." *Time*, April 21. http://time.com/5249811/neo-nazis-burn-swastika-georgia/

Hamilton, J. 2017. "The concert for Charlottesville was a night of stars, tears, and vague platitudes." *Slate*, September 25. www.slate.com/blogs/browbeat/2017/09/25/the_concert_for_charlottesville_reviewed.html

Hankes, K. and Amend, A. 2018. "The alt-right is killing people." *Southern Poverty Law Center Website*, February 5. www.splcenter.org/20180205/alt-right-killing-people

Haslam, N. 2006. "Dehumanization: An integrative review." *Personality and Social Psychology Review*, 10(3): 252–264.

Held, A. 2018. "Shrouds pulled from Charlottesville Confederate statues, following ruling." *NPR*, February 28. www.npr.org/sections/thetwo-way/2018/02/28/589451855/shrouds-pulled-from-charlottesville-confederate-statues-following-ruling

InfoWars. 2018. "Live from Israel: Laura Loomer reports on Iran's missile attack in Golan Heights." *InfoWars*, May 10. www.infowars.com/live-from-israel-laura-loomer-reports-on-irans-missile-attack-in-golan-heights/

Jeltsen, M. 2018. "Far-right activist thrown out Of courthouse at Pulse Nightclub trial." *HuffPost*, March 29. www.huffingtonpost.com/entry/far-right-activist-thrown-out-of-courthouse-at-pulse-nightclub-trial_us_5abd1882e4b06409775e48cb

Kaepernick, C. 2016. *Twitter*, July 7. https://twitter.com/Kaepernick7/status/7510 86182814117888

Kempa, D. 2018. "Chants of 'it's a phone, not a gun' at Sacramento City Hall. . . ." *Periscope*, March. www.pscp.tv/kempadimes/1nAKERDbNEoGL

Kenning, C. 2018. "No charges for Dallas officers who killed sniper with robot bomb." *Reuters*, January 31. www.reuters.com/article/us-texas-crime/no-charges-for-dallas-officers-who-killed-sniper-with-robot-bomb-idUSKBN1FK35W

Kris10. 2018. "NYPD arresting people marching for justice for Stephon Clark." *Periscope*, March. www.pscp.tv/kristensaulina/1PlKQXERdknxE

Lasswell, H. 1938. *Propaganda Technique in the World War*. New York: Peter Smith.

Lasswell, H. and Blumenstock, D. 1939. *World Revolutionary Propaganda: A Chicago Study*. New York: Alfred A. Knopf.

Levant, E. 2017. "Ezra Levant: Why we had to say goodbye to Faith Goldy." *Rebel Media YouTube Video*, August 17. www.youtube.com/watch?v=zz027kdYCls

Light, J. 2018. "Stephon Clark protest #KingsGameLockout." *Periscope*, March. www.pscp.tv/Jlightofficiall/1mrGmRAEkgkJy

Loomer, L. 2017a. "LIVE from the scene of the Islamic terrorist attack in Manhattan." *Periscope*, October 31. www.pscp.tv/LauraLoomer/1MYGNjvrVAnGw

Loomer, L. 2017b. "CNN is ISIS." *Periscope*, October 31. www.pscp.tv/LauraLoomer/1eaJbqDkEdjGX

Loomer, L. 2017c. "Julia Caesar meets Laura Loomer." *Periscope*, June 16. www.pscp.tv/LauraLoomer/1gqxvbVXbrexB

Loomer, L. 2017d. "Crashing Julius Caeser." *Periscope*, June 16. www.pscp.tv/LauraLoomer/1OdJryvRljVGX

Loomer, L. 2018a. *Facebook Page*. www.facebook.com/lauraloomerofficial/

Loomer, L. 2018b. "#JamesComey book tour." *Periscope*, April. www.pscp.tv/w/1DXxyXXaqWNJM?q=laura+loomer

Loomer, L. 2018c. *Twitter Page*, August 2. https://twitter.com/LauraLoomer?lang=en

Loomer, L. 2018d. *Twitter*, May 15. https://twitter.com/LauraLoomer/status/996313342275997696

Loomer, L. 2018e. *Twitter*, August 6. https://twitter.com/LauraLoomer/status/1026530510523310080

Marantz, A. 2017a. "The live-streamers who are challenging traditional journalism." *The New Yorker*, December 11. www.newyorker.com/magazine/2017/12/11/the-live-streamers-who-are-challenging-traditional-journalism

Marantz, A. 2017b. "Behind the scenes with the right-wing activist who crashed 'Julius Caesar'." *The New Yorker*, June 20. www.newyorker.com/news/news-desk/behind-the-scenes-with-the-right-wing-activist-who-crashed-julius-caesar-laura-loomer

Mason, M. 2016. "Michael KB Mason was live." *Facebook Live*, July 7. www.facebook.com/michaelbautista86/videos/899698650159344/

McAuliffe, T. 2017. "Governor McAuliffe statement following Heather Heyer memorial service in Charlottesville." *Periscope*, August 16. www.pscp.tv/w/1PlKQYejOyNKE?q=charlottesville+

McKesson, D. 2016. "#BatonRouge. protest." *Periscope*, July 9. www.pscp. tv/w/1DXxyZjvrWVKM

MPR News. 2016. "Transcript of Facebook video in Philando Castile shooting." *MPR News*, July 7. www.mprnews.org/story/2016/07/07/philando-castile-shooting-video-transcript

Mueller, B. and Schweber, N. 2018. Police fatally shoot a Brooklyn man, saying they thought he had a gun." *The New York Times*, April 4. www.nytimes. com/2018/04/04/nyregion/police-shooting-brooklyn-crown-heights.html

Nicas, J. 2018. "Alex Jones and Infowars content is removed from Apple, Facebook and YouTube." *The New York Times*, August 6. www.nytimes.com/2018/08/06/technology/infowars-alex-jones-apple-facebook-spotify.html

Periscope. 2018. "Community guidelines." *Twitter, Inc.* www.pscp.tv/content

Peters, J. 2001. "Witnessing." *Media, Culture & Society*, 23: 707–723.

Rebel Media. 2018. YouTube Page for Laura Loomer, January 22. www.youtube. com/playlist?list=PL2HWRRSziC_Fxtpn24X8bsg5DS_eL6Z9P

Reuters. 2017. "Uber, Lyft ban conservative activist after anti-Muslim tweets." *CNBC*, November 1. www.cnbc.com/2017/11/01/uber-lyft-ban-activist-laura-loomer-after-anti-muslim-tweets.html

Robles, F. and Del Real, J. 2018. "Stephon Clark was shot 8 times primarily in his back, family-ordered autopsy finds." *The New York Times*, March 30. www. nytimes.com/2018/03/30/us/stephon-clark-independent-autopsy.html

Saslow, E. 2016. "For Diamond Reynolds, trying to move past 10 tragic minutes of video." *The Washington Post*, September 10. www.washingtonpost.com/national/stay-calm-be-patient/2016/09/10/ec4ec3f2-7452-11e6-8149-b8d05321db62_story.html?utm_term=.a284c1d1c710

Spencer, R. 2017a. "Back in Charlottesville." *Periscope*, October 7. www.pscp.tv/w/1yoKMpodMMexQ?q=charlottesville+

Spencer, R. 2017b. "#RichardatUF." *Periscope*, October 19. www.pscp.tv/RichardBSpencer/1zqKVMmjvQlxB

Spencer, R. 2018. *Twitter*, April 27. https://twitter.com/RichardBSpencer/status/989876461128617984

SPLC. undated. "Andrew Anglin." *Southern Poverty Law Center Website*. www. splcenter.org/fighting-hate/extremist-files/individual/andrew-anglin

Stelter, B. 2016. "Philando Castile and the power of Facebook Live." *CNN*, July 7. http://money.cnn.com/2016/07/07/media/facebook-live-streaming-police-shooting/index.html

Stelter, J. 2017. "New York's village Halloween parade." *Spectrum News NY1*, October 31. www.ny1.com/nyc/all-boroughs/news/special-reports/new-york-city-village-halloween-parade

Strange, D. 2017. "Three charged in shooting after Spencer talk." *The Gainesville Sun*, October 20. www.gainesville.com/news/20171020/three-charged-in-shooting-after-spencer-talk

Sullivan, J., Tate, J., and Jenkins, J. 2018. "Fatal police shootings of unarmed people have significantly declined, experts say." *The Washington Post*, May 7. www. washingtonpost.com/investigations/fatal-police-shootings-of-unarmed-people-have-significantly-declined-experts-say/2018/05/03/d5eab374-4349-11e8-8569-26fda6b404c7_story.html?utm_term=.1e749528cfe2

Svrluga, S. and Rozsa, L. 2017. "'Kill them': Three men charged in shooting after Richard Spencer speech." *The Washington Post*, October 20. www.washingtonpost.com/news/grade-point/wp/2017/10/20/kill-them-three-men-charged-in-shooting-after-richard-spencer-speech/?utm_term=.5b3e686f3855

Thijm, Y. A. 2017. "The power of citizen video to create undeniable truths." *TED*, April. www.ted.com/talks/yvette_alberdingk_thijm_the_power_of_citizen_video_to_create_undeniable_truths

Trump, D. 2018a. *Twitter*, May 18. https://twitter.com/realDonaldTrump/status/997429518867591170

Trump, D. 2018b. *Twitter*, June 19. https://twitter.com/realDonaldTrump/status/1009071403918864385?ref_src=twsrc%5Etfw%7Ctwcamp%5Etweetembed%7Ctwterm%5E1009072619805724672&ref_url=http%3A%2F%2Ftime.com%2F5316087%2Fdonald-trump-immigration-infest%2F

Twitter Help Center. 2018. "Verified account FAQs." *Twitter, Inc.* https://help.twitter.com/en/managing-your-account/twitter-verified-accounts

Twitter Safety. 2018. Twitter, September 6. https://twitter.com/TwitterSafety/status/1037804427992686593

Unicorn Riot. 2017. "Unicorn Riot was live." *Facebook Live*, June 16. www.facebook.com/unicornriot.ninja/videos/494680470866179/

Utych, S. 2018. "How dehumanization influences attitudes toward immigrants." *Political Research Quarterly*, 712: 440–452. http://journals.sagepub.com/doi/10.1177/1065912917744897

Wang, F. 2018. "#Sacramento protestors shutting down the freeway for #Stephon-Clark." *Periscope*, March. www.pscp.tv/w/1MYxNpEzwqbGw?q=stephon+clark

Weigel, D. 2017. "Fear of 'violent left' preceded events in Charlottesville." *The Washington Post*, August 13. www.washingtonpost.com/news/powerpost/wp/2017/08/13/fear-of-violent-left-preceded-events-in-charlottesville/?utm_term=.33e599c5f322

Weill, K. and LaPorta, J. 2018. "InfoWars sends professional troll Laura Loomer to Parkland." *Daily Beast*, February 21. www.thedailybeast.com/infowars-sends-professional-troll-laura-loomer-to-parkland

White House. 2018. "The White House was live." *Facebook Live*, May 16. www.facebook.com/WhiteHouse/videos/1680977985323261/

Wilson, J. 2017. "Charlottesville: Man charged with murder was pictured at neo-Nazi rally." *The Guardian*, August 13. www.theguardian.com/us-news/2017/aug/13/charlottesville-james-fields-charged-with-was-pictured-at-neo-nazi-rally-vanguard-america

WMC. 2017. "WMC Action News 5 was live." *Facebook Live*, August 23. www.facebook.com/WMCActionNews5/videos/10154982465837756/

Wyche, S. 2016. "Colin Kaepernick explains why he sat during national anthem." *NFL Media*, August 27. www.nfl.com/news/story/0ap3000000691077/article/colin-kaepernick-explains-why-he-sat-during-national-anthem

Xiong, C. 2017. "Hours after officer Yanez is found not guilty in fatal shooting of Philando Castile, marchers close I-94." *Star Tribune*, June 17. www.startribune.com/fifth-day-of-jury-deliberations-underway-in-yanez-trial/428862473/#1

ziggy. 2018. "ziggy was live." *Periscope*, April 4. www.pscp.tv/w/1vAxRVgOOYVxl

Zuckerberg, M. 2018. "Facebook CEO Mark Zuckerberg: We do not allow hate groups on Facebook | CNBC." *CNBC on YouTube*, April 11. www.youtube.com/watch?v=ABykCSICdy4

4   Politics and live video

Beyond campaigning

While families around the world celebrate Father's Day, demonstrators are marching to Tornillo, Texas. Thousands join virtually, pulling out their phones and tablets to watch the livestreams as the marchers cry, "Free our children now." Democratic Congressman Beto O'Rourke leads the march to a tent city for migrant children, where the U.S. government is holding hundreds of boys, many separated from their parents (O'Rourke 2018a).

Surrounded by protesters, O'Rourke stands out in his crisp powder blue dress shirt, rolling up his sleeves against the heat of the burning Texas sun. A woman on a bullhorn shouts, "What do we want?" He responds with the crowd, "Justice." They continue, "When do we want it?" "Now!" O'Rourke walks along, shaking hands, hugging marchers, and stopping to give interviews, as his team streams on *Facebook Live*. It's shared widely on social media, and by the next day, the views reach nearly three-quarters of a million (2018a).

TV stations are streaming, too. But not every one is actually there at the march. They've picked up a live feed from *CNN* and have posted it to their own *Facebook* pages. The comments are unique to each page, so people watching Pensacola's ABC affiliate, *WEAR*, are interacting with others watching that stream, while viewers of *FOX*'s *KABB* in San Antonio are posting their own comments to that page. Others are streaming *Circa*'s *Facebook Live* feed – *Sinclair Broadcasting*'s digital news service. Add to all of this, video clips shared on social media, embedded into online stories, and reported on broadcast television, and the reach swells. In a sound bite posted by *CBS*, O'Rourke calls out separating migrant families: "This is inhumane. This is cruel. This is torture. To take a child from that mother, from that father – who literally risked all, including their lives, to bring them to safety" (*CBS* quoting O'Rourke 2018).

Meanwhile, another elected official is livestreaming on *Periscope* from the southern tip of Texas, more than 700 miles away. "This is about children being separated from their families, when their families are seeking asylum from persecution abroad," says Senator Jeff Merkley from the border guard station in McAllen (2018a).

In another stream, he walks along the Hidalgo Port of Entry International Bridge toward the Mexico border, and explains what happens when people try to come to the U.S. side. "They can't get across by and large at the official checkpoints, and if they cross at the unofficial checkpoints they're arrested and treated as criminals" (Merkley 2018b).

These livestreams were not the first for Merkley. He drew attention to the child separation issue weeks earlier when he broadcast on *Facebook Live* for nearly 25 minutes, trying to get inside Casa Padre in Brownsville, Texas. He had heard refugee children were being held there, away from their parents. Early in the stream, he walks around a yellow sawhorse marked "KEEP OUT," as he narrates. He then waits at the door to the facility and looks into the camera, saying, "American citizens are funding this operation. And, so every American citizen has a stake in how these children are treated, and how this policy is being enacted." The supervisor eventually meets him – police standing by – and he's then asked to leave (2018c).

Beyond his *Facebook* page, Merkley's livestream flows through other social networks (2018d) and spreads via mainstream media. By late June it has more than 2 million views (2018c).

These live videos have played a key role in drawing attention to the family separation issue, and as *The Washington Post* reported, helped to gain access to Casa Padre. Authorities allowed journalists to tour the facility "amid increased national interest after a U.S. senator, Oregon Democrat Jeff Merkley, was turned away" (Miller, Brown, and Davis 2018).

In addition to livestreams, recorded videos have contributed to the senators' efforts to reveal the truth about migrant children. The march to Tornillo grew out of a video posted to O'Rourke's *Facebook* page, tweeted out just one day before the demonstration. Sunflowers sway in the breeze behind him, as his arms move in rhythm with his words, hands punctuating fervently as he speaks. "I want you to join me tomorrow on Father's Day. And just remember that some of those kids were taken from their fathers at that border" (2018b).

Nimble use of social media amplifies exposure to these messages, sustaining the momentum and connecting events to subsequent action. O'Rourke tweets, "An update since returning from Sunday's march to Tornillo: We've formally introduced legislation that would end the practice of family separation. H.R. 6135 now has over 190 co-sponsors in the House. Companion legislation in the Senate currently has 49 members signed on" (2018c).

Republicans, too, craft a bill. After O'Rourke's march, Senator Ted Cruz announced his own legislation to end migrant family separation, which civil rights attorney Bea Bischoff called a "cynical ploy" (2018).

Perhaps spooked by the response Beto O'Rourke – his Democratic opponent in November's Senate race – received after organizing a march to protest a new tent city being erected for migrant children, Cruz now insists he's concerned for the welfare of the thousands of children currently being held captive in the state he represents.

(Bischoff 2018)

Cruz's social media accounts lend support to Bischoff's assertion. In the days before announcing his bill, his feeds make no reference to the border situation. Instead, they're filled with images of him playing basketball – before, during, and after a charity game against Jimmy Kimmel (Cruz 2018).

While all this is happening, *ProPublica* releases an audio recording made inside a U.S. Customs and Border Protection facility. Children can be heard sobbing desperately as an agent remarks, "We have an orchestra here" (Thompson 2018).

The next day, as protests erupt in D.C. in front of U.S. Customs and Border Protection, an almost surreal livestream emerges. The U.S. Department of State announces it in a tweet (2018a):

Happening soon! Join our colleagues from @TravelGov for a Facebook Live event at 10:00 a.m. ET to ask your questions about traveling with kids and to hear their tips to make traveling with the whole family easier.

A young white male and female host the program. They say she's a mom of three and he's the father of a six-month-old baby girl. He invites viewer interaction: "As we go along, we encourage you guys to comment and ask us questions" (U.S. Department of State 2018b).

Comments flow in quickly, but few pertain to passports.

Simone: *This is astonishingly tone deaf given current events.*
Kristy: *We are keeping children in cages so you make a video about getting passports for Becky and Bobby before the European family vacay?*
Pattie: *Is the bad timing on this "chat" intentional or is the US Dept. of State just so incredibly tone deaf that they don't know that the US is separating children from their parents and holding them in cages? #wherearethegirls*

The male host describes how he held up his baby to take her passport photo. A viewer retorts:

Sarah: *Wow. How sweet you got to hold your daughter, while others' are imprisoned. Awesome!*

Comments about the migrant detention centers keep coming, with no acknowledgment from the hosts.

> Melissa: *This is unbelievable. Every single day I'm amazed at what this administration does. Two white people talking about the privileges they enjoy when traveling with children. You make me ill.*
> Mike: *Could you please give me tips on how to not have my young daughter stolen from me at the border if I don't have the exact right paperwork on hand?*

At least one viewer is bothered by the negativity.

> Jamie: *Wow – leave the video if you aren't interested in getting a US passport for your kids. Some of us actually need information . . .*

The hosts wrap up the stream by holding up their babies' passport photos as they sign out (U.S. Department of State 2018b).

Whether this was simply bad timing, or something more, the *Facebook Live* event showcases public discontent with U.S. immigration policy. Journalists quickly pick up on the citizen disapproval and post stories, including comments from the livestream.

Opposition to family separation continues to swell, and just three days after the march to Tornillo, livestreams across the country reveal crowds flooding streets and government buildings. Demonstrators in Boston (*WBZ* 2018) and Kansas City (*Fox4* 2018) protest, while U.S. House Democrats decry the Trump administration's "heartless, cruel, and dangerous family separation policy" (Nadler 2018).

And then, a development in the White House unfolds and news media livestream the moment Donald Trump signs an executive order to keep migrant families together. As he picks up his pen, he remarks, "OK, you're gonna have a lot of happy people" (*ABC News* 2018).

O'Rourke and Merkley take to social media soon after. Merkley credits the public's outcry and pressure for the action, but is not satisfied with the plan, calling it "handcuffs for all" (2018e). O'Rourke tweets, "Let's immediately reunite separated families" (2018d).

The lawmakers' deft social media use, video, and livestreaming played a central role in illuminating this issue and their part in it. As human rights organization, Witness.org writes, "filming matters" (2018).

But O'Rourke is no stranger to social media livestreaming. In fact, he was one of the early pioneers of this technology among his peers in Congress.[1]

Early livestreams from politicians

Ten days after the Pulse Nightclub Shooting that killed 49 in Orlando, Florida, U.S. House Democrats were demanding action on gun control. They staged a sit-in, but when speaker Paul Ryan deemed the House in recess, the *C-SPAN* cameras were turned off. So, the House members themselves made their own livestreams. Beto O'Rourke opened up *Facebook Live* (2016), and soon *CNN* (2016) and *BuzzFeed News* (2016) placed his feed onto their pages.

Scott Peters of California streamed on *Periscope* for the first time. *The Guardian* reported that Peters downloaded the app on the House floor after one of his staff suggested Periscoping the sit-in (Woolf 2016).

Another nascent livestream came months before the sit-in, using the service *UStream*. Kentucky Senator Rand Paul's team broadcast a day on the Iowa campaign trail live in October 2015. He appeared less than enthusiastic, however. As the sun sets behind him, he reads questions posted on the Internet.

> Third question, most popular question from Google is, "Is Rand Paul still running for president?" And, I don't know, I wouldn't be doin' this dumbass livestreaming if I weren't. Yes, I still am running for president. Get over it.
>
> (Paul video clip in Bump 2015)

This followed an earlier *Periscope* broadcast with a journalist for *The Guardian* – one of the first livestreams on social media with a presidential candidate. When Paul Lewis asked Rand Paul about polling numbers, the senator simply walked out of frame, ending the interview. Moments later, as Lewis went on camera to explain what had happened, the lights went out. In an interview about the incident, Lewis said, "He wasn't treating it in the way he would a more conventional broadcast," and that "It reflected somewhat badly on him" (Lewis quoted in Artwick 2018).

Today, broadcasting live on social media has become a key element for lawmakers in communicating with constituents, by calling attention to issues and addressing them, and by mobilizing action.

SOTU

The tradition of broadcasting the U.S. State of the Union began in 1923 when President Calvin Coolidge went live from the House chamber, on "six powerful radio stations." More than 1 million people listened, which was at that time "more people than the voice of any man in history" (*The New York Times* 1923). Fast forward to 2018, when livestreams on *YouTube, Facebook*, and *Periscope* brought Donald Trump's SOTU to viewers world-wide. Some even incorporated fundraising into the mix. The Republication National Committee and Official Team Trump *Periscope* accounts ran the feed with a red, white, and blue ticker at the bottom of the screen, displaying names, states, and dollar amounts. An email sent to supporters before the speech invited them to donate, even as little as one dollar, to have their name displayed during the livestream (Criss 2018). Some critics found the ticker unsavory. Others questioned its ethics. Watchdog organization Public Citizen filed a complaint against speaker Paul Ryan for allowing the livestream to be used for partisan purposes (2018).

But myriad viewing options were available during the event, including mainstream media livestreams. And immediately afterward, the House Democrats (2018) broadcast Joe Kennedy III giving the official response live on *Periscope*. Still others went live with their own messages, including Maxine Waters via *BET* and Bernie Sanders on *Facebook Live*.

It wasn't the first time Sanders used the platform to respond to a Trump speech.

He streamed live on *Facebook* in 2017 after Trump's first address to Congress. That livestream grew out of his success with the interview program, "The Bernie Sanders Show," which was just getting started on *Facebook* at the time. After his show's live broadcast with Bill Nye garnered more than 4 million views, his staff sensed "an opportunity." They turned down multiple television requests for the Trump response, instead going directly to Sanders' *Facebook* page (Debenedetti 2018). Their intuition paid off, with 8.5 million views for that first response (Sanders 2017). *New York* magazine writes that Sanders is "quietly building a digital media empire" (Debenedetti 2018). Livestreams feature prominently, bringing events directly to constituents, such as his "Medicare for All" on *Facebook Live*. He called it "historic," as the first senate town meeting to take place outside corporate media (Sanders 2018). "So tonight, let me guarantee you that this event will not be interrupted by commercials from the drug companies or Wall Street or the insurance companies" (Sanders 2018).

In addition to unfiltered communication is interactivity – a major characteristic of livestreaming on social media. Not only does the comment function allow viewers to post about the content, share it, and interact with others, but in its most open form, it offers the potential to engage with the host. While Sanders brought in questions via video, the *Facebook* comments were not moderated, nor were they included in the livestreamed discussion. Nonetheless, viewers did respond to the panelists, and interact with one another in the comments, contributing to the discussion and democratic process. A true virtual town hall would also engage the livestream viewers by inviting them to comment and responding to them during the event.

Livestream levels of engagement

Livestream as lecture, comments disabled

The host delivers a speech or narrates as an event unfolds. Viewers have no opportunity to interact.

Livestream as forum for discussion, comments enabled

Enabling comments allows the viewers to discuss what they're seeing and hearing in real time. The host does not acknowledge the virtual viewers, however, and the comments are not monitored.

Virtual town hall

The host welcomes viewers to comment and responds to them. Often, another person assists the livestreamer by monitoring and pinning comments to be addressed. While this offers the highest level of engagement, it also opens the door to trolling and hate speech, as trolls or bots seek to disrupt.

#MeToo

In 2005, Rachel Crooks encountered Donald Trump outside an elevator in Trump Tower where she worked. The 22-year-old receptionist introduced herself and shook his hand, but he would not let go, she said, and went on to kiss her cheeks and mouth (Haag 2018). She went public with her accusation during the 2016 presidential election, and in May 2018 joined a "national surge of female political newcomers" by winning the Democratic primary for an Ohio House of Representatives seat (Haag 2018).

Before Crooks announced her intent to run for office, she appeared in a livestreamed event related to #MeToo. In it, three women with somber faces sit at a table waiting for their chance to speak. The two millennials and a baby boomer, while separated by generations, are united in what they're about to say – and do. They're about to share unsettling experiences with a roomful of journalists and a global audience watching the livestream. It's the second time that day the women would tell their stories. Earlier that morning, Rachel Crooks, Samantha Holvey, and Jessica Leeds appeared on the

Megyn Kelly Today show to discuss Donald Trump and sexual misconduct (Kelly 2017).

The news briefing dovetailed with the Kelly interview, and was promoted as a plea for Congressional action against Trump. More than a year had passed since the women first publicly shared their accounts of Trump's unwanted presence and physical advances against them – being groped on an airplane, ogled in a dressing room, and kissed on the mouth in his office building.

As the women spoke, a wall-sized banner behind them was ever present, announcing in red capital letters, "BRAVE NEW FILMS."

Producer Shira Levine helped arrange the news conference, reaching out to the women, "so they could tell their stories again, this time in the context of and in support of the #MeToo movement" (Levine 2017).

In the Q&A, Renita Young of *Reuters* asked if the women were seeking a Congressional investigation (*PBS News* 2017). Crooks answered, "If they were willing to investigate Senator Franken, I think it's only fair that they do the same for Trump" (*PBS News* 2017).

That same day, Democratic Senator Kirsten Gillibrand of New York appeared on *CNN*. "President Trump should resign," she told Christiane Amanpour. "These allegations are credible; they are numerous. I've heard these women's testimony, and many of them are heartbreaking" (*CNN* 2017).

Trump tweeted the following morning:

> Lightweight Senator Kirsten Gillibrand, a total flunky for Chuck Schumer and someone who would come to my office 'begging' for campaign contributions not so long ago (and would do anything for them), is now in the ring fighting against Trump. Very disloyal to Bill & Crooked-USED!
>
> (2017)

She tweeted back within the hour, "You cannot silence me or the millions of women who have gotten off the sidelines to speak out about the unfitness and shame you have brought to the Oval Office" (Gillibrand 2017).

Later that day, a dozen Democrats in Congress held their own news conference at the U.S. Capitol Visitor Center. "The MeToo movement has arrived," begins Lois Frankel.

> Sexual abuse will not be tolerated, whether it's by a Hollywood producer, chef of a restaurant, and member of Congress, or the president of the United States. No man or woman is above the law. #MeToo is saying loud and clear that accusations of sexual abuse should be taken seriously.
>
> (*C-Span* 2017)

They announced their formal letter to the Oversight & Government Reform committee, signed by more than 100 legislators, calling for a congressional investigation into the allegations of sexual misconduct by Donald J. Trump. "Simply said," Frankel adds, "Americans deserve the truth" (*C-Span* 2017).

Mainstream news coverage directly connected the congressional response and the previous day's news conference, including a photo in some stories (Nilsen 2017; Viebeck 2018; Wire 2017).

But the Brave New Films' livestream was not the first to bring together accusers of a politician's sexual misconduct. A prominent *Facebook Live* broadcast took place during the election, just hours before the second debate. That was two days after the *Access Hollywood* tape revealed Trump making vulgar comments against women (Fahrenthold 2016). In what appeared as a move to divert attention away from the tape, Trump hosted a *Facebook Live* broadcast, bringing together several women who had made accusations against former President Bill Clinton. Trump's livestream garnered nearly 4 million views (Trump 2016). It opens with him seated at a table with two women on either side, an American flag behind them. The camera pans over as Steve Bannon and about a dozen others walk in, some wearing press passes. There's a professional-sized video camera in the room, but the livestream video is amateurish, a bit shaky and not miked. It pans back over to Trump. "These four very courageous women have asked to be here, and it was our honor to help them," says Trump. Each woman then speaks briefly, professing their support for him. Accusations are made against Bill and Hillary Clinton. As Trump wraps it up, a male reporter shouts, "Why did you say you touched women without consent, Mr. Trump?" Paula Jones yells back, "Why don't you go ask Bill Clinton that? Go ahead, ask Hillary as well." The room breaks out in applause (Trump 2016). Later, the accusers attended the debate. CNN reports the Clinton campaign was "jarred by the news" (Diaz and Zeleny 2016).

Women's studies scholar Ashwini Tambe sees Trump's election as a likely trigger for #MeToo: "Trump's impunity has, I suggest, provoked the impatience and fury at the heart of this movement" (2017). She argues, "For many, Trump represents the ultimate unpunished sexual predator." That, she says, has led to a "collective emboldening," and what she calls "horizontal action." She draws this term from Freire's concept of horizontal violence, which involves "substituting a difficult powerful target with a more accessible one like peers or kin. The large numbers of victims naming colleagues for sexual harassment suggests 'an awakening'" (Tambe 2017).

Social media livestreaming appears to be facilitating this "horizontal action," providing yet another space for women to express their #MeToo experiences and opinions. In her acceptance speech at the Golden Globe Awards, Oprah Winfrey acknowledged the power of speaking truth.

> For too long, women have not been heard or believed if they dared to speak their truth to the power of those men. But their time is up. (*explosive applause*) Their time is up! Their time is up.
>
> (Winfrey 2018)

Note

1 O'Rourke's team multi-purposed his livestreams in 2018, creating a campaign ad using footage shot with an iPhone and drawn from the live video of his travels to 254 Texas counties (O'Rourke 2018e).

References

ABC News. 2018. "ABC News special report: Pres. Trump signs executive order on family separation." *Periscope*, June 20. www.pscp.tv/w/1ynJOYQlZozKR

Artwick, C. 2018. "Social media livestreaming." In S. Eldridge II and B. Franklin, Eds., *The Routledge Handbook of Developments in Digital Journalism Studies*. Abingdon: Routledge.

Bischoff, B. 2018. "Ted Cruz's proposal to fix child separation is a cynical ploy." *Slate*, June 19. https://slate.com/news-and-politics/2018/06/ted-cruzs-protect-kids-and-parents-act-is-a-cynical-ploy.html

Bump, P. 2015. "Rand Paul's 'dumbass' masochistic campaign gimmick." *The Washington Post*, October 14. www.washingtonpost.com/news/the-fix/wp/2015/10/14/rand-pauls-masochistic-campaign-gimmick/?utm_term=.adab15791926

BuzzFeed News. 2016. "BuzzFeed News was live." *Facebook Live*, June 22. www.facebook.com/BuzzFeedNews/videos/1176172252403791

CBS Quoting O'Rourke. 2018. "CBS News is at Texas." *Facebook*, June 17. www.facebook.com/CBSNews/videos/10155883930770950/

CNN. 2016. "CNN was live." *Facebook Live*, June 22. www.facebook.com/cnn/videos/democrats-stage-sit-in-for/10154949772731509/

CNN. 2017. "CNN exclusive: Sen. Kirsten Gillibrand calls on Trump to resign." *CNN*, December 11. www.cnn.com/2017/12/11/politics/trump-resign-gillibrand-sexual-assault/index.html

Criss, D. 2018. "For $1, the Trump campaign will include your name on its SOTU livestream." *CNN*, January 30. www.cnn.com/2018/01/30/politics/trump-campaign-state-of-the-union-donation-trnd/index.html

Cruz, T. 2018. *Twitter*, June 19. https://twitter.com/tedcruz/status/1009062637404131328

C-SPAN. 2017. "House democrats on sexual misconduct allegations against president." *C-SPAN*, December 12. www.c-span.org/video/?438499-1/house-democrats-call-investigation-sexual-misconduct-allegations-president

Debenedetti, G. 2018. "Bernie sanders is quietly building a digital media empire." *New York*, April 22. http://nymag.com/daily/intelligencer/2018/04/bernie-sanders-is-quietly-building-a-digital-media-empire.html

Diaz, D. and Zeleny, J. 2016. "Trump appears with Bill Clinton accusers before debate." *CNN*, October 10. www.cnn.com/2016/10/09/politics/donald-trump-juanita-broaddrick-paula-jones-facebook-live-2016-election/index.html

Fahrenthold, D. 2016. "Trump recorded having extremely lewd conversation about women in 2005." *The Washington Post*, October 8. www.washingtonpost.com/politics/trump-recorded-having-extremely-lewd-conversation-about-women-in-2005/2016/10/07/3b9ce776-8cb4-11e6-bf8a-3d26847eeed4_story.html?utm_term=.f49a1f2a5f99

Fox4. 2018. "FOX 4 News Kansas City was live." *Facebook Live*, June 20. www.facebook.com/fox4kc/videos/10155979716808645/

Gillibrand, K. 2017. *Twitter*, December 12. https://twitter.com/SenGillibrand/status/940580340560809984?ref_src=twsrc%5Etfw&ref_url=http%3A%2F%2Fdeadline.com%2F2017%2F12%2Fdonald-trump-kirsten-gillibrand-sex-for-contributions-response-harassment-resign-twitter-1202225061%2F

Haag, M. 2018. "Rachel Crooks, who accused Trump of sexual assault, wins legislative primary." *The New York Times*, May 19. www.nytimes.com/2018/05/09/us/politics/rachel-crooks-ohio.html

House Democrats. 2018. "Watch live as @RepJoeKennedy delivers the response to #SOTU." *Periscope*, January 30. www.pscp.tv/HouseDemocrats/1OyKAdjmZMgxb

Kelly, M. 2017. "3 women who have accused Trump of sexual misconduct join Megyn Kelly." *Today*, December 11. www.today.com/video/3-women-who-have-accused-trump-of-sexual-misconduct-join-megyn-kelly-1113822787644

Levine, S. 2017. "I helped organize the Trump accusers press conference: Here's why we did it." *Fortune*, December 15. http://fortune.com/2017/12/15/donald-trump-sexual-assault-accusations-jessica-leeds/

Lewis, P. 2018. In Artwick.

Merkley, J. 2018a. "Back at the border, on Father's Day, investigating @realdonaldtrump child snatching policy." *Periscope*, June 17. www.pscp.tv/w/1ZkJzNPajkRJv

Merkley, J. 2018b. "We're on the Hidalgo Port of Entry International Bridge." *Periscope*, June 17. www.pscp.tv/w/1ynJOYQnrbEKR

Merkley, J. 2018c. "Senator Jeff Merkley was live." *Facebook Live*, June 3. www.facebook.com/jeffmerkley/videos/10155510407061546/

Merkley, J. 2018d. *Twitter*, June 3. https://twitter.com/SenJeffMerkley/status/1003396188459143170

Merkley, J. 2018e. *Twitter*, June 20. https://twitter.com/SenJeffMerkley/status/1009589901845778437

Miller, M., Brown, E., and Davis, A. 2018. "Inside Casa Padre, the converted Walmart where the U.S. is holding nearly 1,500 immigrant children." *The Washington Post*, June 14. www.washingtonpost.com/local/inside-casa-padre-the-converted-walmart-where-the-us-is-holding-nearly-1500-immigrant-children/2018/06/14/0cd65ce4-6eba-11e8-bd50-b80389a4e569_story.html?utm_term=.81ee3d3c1dac

Nadler, J. 2018. "House democrats speak on immigration after Trump said he'd sign an executive order to keep families together." *BuzzFeed News Periscope*, June 20. www.pscp.tv/w/1jMJgEbBQVyKL?q=buzzfeed+news

The New York Times. 1923. "A million persons will hear Coolidge's voice when he addresses Congress this afternoon." *The New York Times*, December 5. https://archive.nytimes.com/www.nytimes.com/learning/general/onthisday/big/1206.html#article

Nilsen, E. 2017. "More than 100 members of Congress want the Oversight Committee to investigate Trump." *Vox*, December 12. www.vox.com/policy-and-politics/2017/12/12/16766800/democratic-congress-members-trump-investigation-women

O'Rourke, B. 2016. "Congressman Beto O'Rourke was live." *Facebook Live*, June 22. www.facebook.com/BetoORourkeTX16/videos/1187449984654186/

O'Rourke, B. 2018a. "Beto O'Rourke was live." *Facebook Live*, June 17. www.facebook.com/betoorourke/videos/1684365804946456/

O'Rourke, B. 2018b. "Beto O'Rourke." *Facebook*, June 16. www.facebook.com/betoorourke/videos/1683103665072670/

O'Rourke, B. 2018c. *Twitter*, June 19. https://twitter.com/betoorourke/status/1009177580635873280?lang=en

O'Rourke, B. 2018d. *Twitter*, June 20. https://twitter.com/BetoORourke/status/1009528339684470785

O'Rourke, B. 2018e. *Twitter*, July 26. https://twitter.com/betoorourke/status/1022466953288593409?lang=en

Paul, R. 2015. Video clip in Bump.

PBS News. 2017. "WATCH: Trump sexual misconduct accusers hold news briefing." *YouTube Livestream*, December 11. www.youtube.com/watch?v=N4LQuwSjc34

Public Citizen. 2018. "Public Citizen files complaint against speaker Ryan for Allowing floor broadcasts to be used for partisan campaigns." *Public Citizen Website*, January 31. www.citizen.org/media/press-releases/public-citizen-files-complaint-against-speaker-ryan-allowing-floor-broadcasts

Sanders, B. 2017. "U.S. Senator Bernie Sanders was live." *Facebook Live*, February 28. www.facebook.com/senatorsanders/videos/10155681411947908/

Sanders, B. 2018. "U.S. Senator Bernie Sanders was live." *Facebook Live*, January 23. www.facebook.com/senatorsanders/videos/10156695924547908/

Tambe, A. 2017. "Has Trump's presidency triggered the movement against sexual harassment?" *The Conversation*, November 28. https://theconversation.com/has-trumps-presidency-triggered-the-movement-against-sexual-harassment-88219

Thompson, G. 2018. "Listen to children who've just been separated from their parents at the border." *ProPublica*, June 18. www.propublica.org/article/children-separated-from-parents-border-patrol-cbp-trump-immigration-policy

Trump, D. 2016. "Donald J. Trump was live." *Facebook Live*, October 9. www.facebook.com/DonaldTrump/videos/10157857037430725/

Trump, D. 2017. *Twitter*, December 12. https://twitter.com/realdonaldtrump/status/940567812053053441?lang=en

U.S. Department of State. 2018a. *Twitter*, June 19. https://twitter.com/StateDept/status/1009071525234987008

U.S. Department of State. 2018b. "U.S. Department of State: Consular Affairs was live." *Facebook Live*, June 19. www.facebook.com/travelgov/videos/10156399914598149/

Viebeck, E. 2018. "Female Democrats plan sexual harassment protest for Trump's State of the Union." *The Washington Post*, January 10. www.washingtonpost. com/powerpost/female-democrats-plan-sexual-harassment-protest-for-trumps-state-of-the-union/2018/01/10/0f0c568e-f61b-11e7-a9e3-ab18ce41436a_story. html?utm_term=.f78a77e2fc96

WBZ. 2018. "Right now: A large crowd at the Massachusetts Statehouse is protesting the separation of immigrant children from their families at the border." *Facebook*, June 20. www.facebook.com/CBSBoston/videos/10156574130042010/

Winfrey, O. 2018. "Oprah Winfrey receives Cecil B. de Mille award at the 2018 Golden Globes." *NBC Video on YouTube*, January 7. www.youtube.com/ watch?v=fN5HV79_8B8

Wire, S. 2017. "Female lawmakers call for investigation into Trump sexual misconduct allegations." *Los Angeles Times*, December 12. www.latimes.com/politics/ washington/la-na-pol-essential-washington-updates-female-lawmakers-call-for-investigation-1513104808-htmlstory.html

Witness.org. 2018. "Eyes on the border: Keeping families together." *Witness Media Lab*. https://lab.witness.org/eyes-on-the-border-keeping-families-together/

Woolf, N. 2016. "Democrats stream gun control sit-in on Periscope after Republicans turn TV cameras off." *The Guardian*, June 23. www.theguardian.com/ technology/2016/jun/22/democrats-sit-in-periscope-facebook-live-gun-control

5   Ethical and legal issues

Prentis Robinson held a selfie stick as he walked away from the police station in Wingate, North Carolina. He had just reported a stolen cell phone and was streaming on *Facebook Live*. "I'm going to move from here," he says. "Going to Atlanta. Charlotte ain't far enough." Suddenly startled, as someone approaches, Robinson says to the person, "You *on* live." He repeats, "You *on* live." And again, "You *on* live." The fourth time, he shouts, "You on *live*," as he swings the camera around to reveal a man in a dark jacket holding what appears to be a handgun. Those were Robinson's last words, as a moment later, the man shot and killed him on the livestream (Perez 2018; *NBC News* 2018).[1]

Crime, violence, and livestreaming

Sadly, stories like these have become more frequent, as violence in real life is delivered to our screens on *Facebook*, *Periscope*, and *YouTube*. Robinson's death and others were unintentionally livestreamed, like the fatal shooting of a two-year-old boy and his uncle on Chicago's West Side (*Chicago Tribune* 2018). Other crimes have been deliberately livestreamed, including a gang rape (Rosenberg-Douglas 2017) and the kidnapping and torture of a disabled teen (Schmadeke 2017). Criticism and public outrage followed each horrific episode.

But the tipping point came when murderers took to streaming on *Facebook*. On Easter Sunday, 2017, a killer made a video as he fatally shot a man at random on a street in Cleveland. The victim, 74-year-old grandfather Robert Godwin Jr., "just happened to walk into the path of the deranged gunman" (Morice 2017). The killer posted the video to his *Facebook* page and then livestreamed as he talked about it. "I shamed myself," the killer said in the livestream. "I snapped. . . . I just killed 13 motherf******, man. . . . I'm about to keep killing until they catch me, f*** it" (Morice 2017).

Not more than a week later, a young man in Thailand killed his 11-month-old baby daughter on *Facebook Live*. The video remained online for about 20 hours, and had more than a quarter-million views (Mozur 2017). *The New York Times* reported:

> The video showed Mr. Wongtalay fixing a noose around his daughter's neck and then dropping her off the side of a building. After a burst of crying, he climbed over the side to retrieve her body. His subsequent suicide was not shown online.
>
> (Mozur 2017)

Facebook took action following the two killings, adding 3,000 people to the 4,500 already in place to monitor content. Mark Zuckerberg posted to his *Facebook* page that seeing "people hurting themselves and others on Facebook" was "heartbreaking." And, *Facebook* said they were working on tools to simplify processes for reporting problems, identifying violations, and contacting police (2017).

The public found the videos distressing as well. A random snapshot of 500 tweets following the Cleveland shooting revealed "video" and "instead" as the top terms being used on the platform. People were responding to a plea from Godwin's grandson to retweet photos of the victim and his family, to honor his grandfather's life, instead of perpetuating the horror of his death by sharing links to the video (*twXplorer* 2017).

"Please please please stop retweeting that video and report anyone who has posted it! That is my grandfather show some respect #Cleveland" (Godwin, in Hurst 2017). Virginia lawmaker Chris Hurst was among those who honored the request. Several years earlier, the former anchorman had seen his girlfriend killed during a live television broadcast. When he retweeted Ryan Godwin's posting, he added, "I know that cry and hope more listen to you than they did to me" (Hurst 2017).

Hurst was making reference to a video the killer made as he murdered reporter Alison Parker and cameraman Adam Ward during a live television broadcast (Shear, Perez-Pena, and Blinder 2015).

"I filmed the shooting see Facebook," the killer tweeted (screen shot of shooter's *Twitter* feed 2015). Journalists posted the killer's account name and tweeted their reactions, such as, "Dear. Lord." and "I want to vomit" (screenshots of author's *Twitter* feed 2015). And they warned, "Don't watch it people, don't watch it."

Some blame these violent acts, in part, on social media platforms and digital tools and technology, including livestreaming. Others argue that news organizations and journalists are complicit in perpetuating the public violence. Following the shooting at *YouTube*'s headquarters in San Bruno, California, major news organizations headlined the perpetrator as the "You-Tube Shooter" (Yan and Karimi 2018; Eordogh 2018; Roberts 2018). *The New York Times*' video, "Who was the YouTube shooter?" features an array of clips from the woman's video channels (Schick and Erdbrink 2018).

Coverage of other killings used monikers as well, such as "Virginia Shooter," or the "WDBJ shooter." And in the Cleveland incident, "Facebook Killer" was used repeatedly and persisted through the month following the murder (Gingras 2017; Remington 2017). Poynter media ethicist Kelly McBride encourages journalists to resist using nicknames for notorious criminals, because they can "cause harm" (2017). That harm can include "contagion," increasing the potential for shootings as well as suicides (2017).

Research puts the time frame for contagion at about two weeks. One study found "significant evidence that mass killings involving firearms are incented by similar events in the immediate past" (Towers et al. 2015). Another concluded that perhaps "the spectacle of recent active shootings contributes to the tragic crystallization of long-simmering active shooting plans" (Kissner 2016, 58).

In addition to nicknaming criminals, other practices can lead to "generalized imitation," include naming and showing images of the killer, discussing the killer's life, and providing details of the violent event (Meindl and Ivy 2017). News media often employ these practices when they cover mass shootings, which may confer notoriety and social status upon the shooter (Meindl and Ivy 2017).

Livestreamed murders and other violent acts create a conundrum for journalists and news organizations. How can they cover these egregious acts without inciting further violence or harm? They must grapple with the ramifications of including the brutal images that may already be publicly available via social media and digital video. Should they embed the full video, clips, or screenshots into their own stories? Should they name the perpetrator or include details about the person or the violent act? If others are already reporting these details and images, does that mean it's OK to do the same? Turning to the SPJ Code of Ethics can help, such as the statement – often tweeted during breaking news – "Avoid pandering to lurid curiosity, even if others do" (2014).

"Do your job and don't cause unjustified harm," is another guideline, otherwise known as the "ethics mantra" (Lester 2018, preface). Harm can take many forms, and may not be apparent until it's taken a toll. For example, while covering the mass shooting in Parkland, Florida, news helicopters flew overhead, livestreaming above the scene and later, at rallies and even memorial services. Some of the survivors conveyed their pain on social media. Before returning to school, Emma González tweeted, "Please, so many of us are suffering from PTSD (it's only made things worse for those who live close to school). The only thing that should be over head are the souls of our dearly departed Eagles" (2018).

Along with respect comes a concern for safety. In the heat of breaking news, journalists chasing the story may find themselves pushing too hard to interact with sources on the scene. Smartphones and social media can facilitate this, connecting journalists with people during lockdowns and other tenuous situations. During the *Annapolis Capital Gazette* shooting, after an intern tweeted, "Active shooter 888 Bestgate please help us," numerous news organizations responded, asking for an interview (Grueskin 2018). Columbia Journalism School Professor Bill Grueskin called attention to this, tweeting, "TV reporters respond to him with the same mix of 'hope you're ok' and 'hope you talk to me'" (2018), which was met with both criticism for media bashing and support for the practice as legitimate newsgathering.

Whether seeking an interview or permission for user-generated content, the safety of those on the scene should take priority, as the Online News Association suggests in its project, *Build Your Own Ethics Code*:

> News organizations need to consider when simply contacting a member of the public in search of UGC might put them in danger, because it might reveal their presence on the scene, or because the simple act of communicating might distract them from staying safe. Sometimes it's best to wait until after the danger has passed.
>
> (ONA 2018)

Other forms of harm can take place well after the incident. Livestreaming the suspected perpetrator appearing in court, or releasing information about the person as it later surfaces may also harm the survivors. News media repeatedly named the accused gunman that killed 17 people at Marjory Stoneman Douglas High School. Livestreams of his first court appearance were viewed widely. Subsequently, he's received "volumes of fan mail" (Rosenberg 2018), which concerns Broward County Public Defender Howard Finkelstein. "The letters shake me up because they are written by regular, everyday teenage girls from across the nation," (quoted in Rosenberg 2018).

After police released videos made by the shooter, survivor Cameron Kasky wrote,

> If the media is going to circulate photos or videos of school shooters, they NEED TO START ADDING WARNINGS. There are people (like

me) who are truly shaken by looking at the shooter and using their names and images creates the notoriety that many of them seek.

(2018)

In some cases, news media and law enforcement officials have refused to name the perpetrator. After the Pulse nightclub shooting in Orlando, James Comey, who was FBI director at the time, would not speak the gunman's name during a live news conference. "'You will notice that I am not using the killer's name, and I will try not to do that,' Comey said during the live news conference," reported the Associated Press (Gurman 2016). "'I don't want to be part of that for the sake of the victims and their families,' Comey said, 'and so that other twisted minds don't think that this is a path to fame and recognition'" (Gurman 2016).

Journalists covering the 2018 Florida video game tournament shooting publicly debated naming the suspect during their reporting process. *Los Angeles Times* reporter Matt Pearce responded to criticism on *Twitter* for including the name:

> I know people have strong feelings about this, but I also spent several hours watching a bunch of people on Twitter 100% identify the wrong guy. I'm not a fan of giant photos of the suspect, etc., but at some level my job is to provide detail and clarity.

(2018)

Lois Beckett of *The Guardian* responded, "To be clear: the advocates who founded the #NoNotoriety campaign *do not* argue that journalists should *never* name the shooter. Their guidelines state that names should be used sparingly, and not in headlines/other prominent ways" (2018).

Others propose taking action. "Any media organizations that insist on continuing to give mass shooters the fame they want should face public censure unless and until they change their ways" (Lankford and Madfis 2018).

Livestreaming suicide

At least a dozen suicides had been livestreamed on social media between May 2016 and May 2018. They included adolescent girls who interacted with viewers before killing themselves (Miller and Burch 2017), a man with bipolar disorder who set himself on fire (McCausland 2017), and a teen boy involved in the "Dangerous Viral 'Blue Whale Challenge' That Targets Kids" (Herron 2017). In some cases, viewers had alerted authorities, who then intervened in suicide attempts during livestreams (Mann 2017). Being there to listen can serve to help. But, viewers can also exacerbate the situation by inadvertently saying something offensive or even by purposely goading the person to "do it."

Before the digital era, standard newsroom policy had been simply to not cover suicides. But today, drama and images are thrust into the public eye via social media, and journalists must now grapple with how to handle each new case of self-harm. Stories that explicitly describe the method, use graphic images, glamorize death, or sensationalize it increase the risk of additional suicides (reportingonsuicide.org 2015).

Facebook offers an online form for reporting suicide (2016) and uses artificial intelligence "to help identify when someone might be expressing thoughts of suicide, including on Facebook Live" (Rosen 2017). *The Guardian* reports, "Facebook will allow users to livestream attempts to self-harm because it 'doesn't want to censor or punish people in distress who are attempting suicide'" (Hopkins 2017). The community guidelines for *Periscope* tell users to not post self-harm or suicide, but if someone does, say they may reach out to help (2017).

Journalists could help minimize harm in future instances of livestreamed suicide by avoiding sensationalized coverage, including resource information, and using family photos instead of images from the scene (reporting on suicide.org 2015).

Privacy

A number of privacy issues emerge with livestreaming. The first concerns the personal information associated with our accounts and how social media companies use it. The second involves the video camera in our phones that can almost seamlessly move with us wherever we go, broadcasting live whatever and whoever might be in its path.

As news of *Facebook* sharing user data with Cambridge Analytica surfaced, the company's COO, Sheryl Sandberg, offered an apology. In an interview with *NPR*'s Steve Inskeep, Sandberg said, "We know that we did not do enough to protect people's data. I'm really sorry for that, Mark's really sorry for that. And what we're doing now is taking really firm action" (Sandberg, quoted in Inskeep 2018). That action included giving users easy access to their privacy settings and control of app data sharing. She also said they should have taken these steps years ago, but explained, "We were way too idealistic. We did not think enough about the abuse cases" (Sandberg, quoted in Inskeep 2018).

The practice of corporations collecting our data has been coined "surveillance capitalism," which Hollywood film director Oliver Stone cited in a 2016 Comic-Con panel. At the time, Pokémon Go had just been launched, and the audience laughed when someone mentioned the game. But Stone was serious. "It's not really funny. What's happening is a new level of invasion," said Stone, as reported by *Time Magazine* (Stone quoted in Dockterman 2016).

The company had been collecting personal data on users, going well beyond basic information. Many of us accept data sharing as the norm, even though we may not like it. But, it's what we *don't* expect that bothers the champions for mobile and online privacy. For example, *Snapchat* can collect information about you from your friend's device's phonebook, and combine it with other information about you. That's without your permission, if your friend grants *Snapchat* access.

This is the kind of information stated in the user agreements for our social media accounts. But when installing apps, how many people click "OK" rather than read the fine print? Being aware of these practices and monitoring our privacy settings can be a first step toward protecting our personal data.

Smartphone cameras and privacy

Social media livestreaming may be reshaping the way we think about privacy and the right to record in public (Stewart and Littau 2016). The pervasiveness of video recording may be serving to normalize it. Because video is so commonplace, objections are difficult to pursue "against the force of reasonable expectation" (Nissenbaum 2009, 161). In the past, privacy could be affected by the separate actions of collection and dissemination. Now, they can be done concurrently through livestreaming on social media, which can increase "the potential for harm that cannot be undone" (Stewart and Littau 2016, 317).

In addition, commenting during livestreaming allows for interaction in real time. Protection against defamation had been provided via Section 230 of the U.S. Communications Decency Act for reader comments posted to news stories (Reporters Committee undated). But, would that protection carry over to comments on the livestream platform? Other regulation may come from individual state laws related to recording and eavesdropping (Stewart and Littau 2016), and by corporations through their own policies for privacy and use of service.

Using others' livestreamed content

What rights do livestreamers have over their content, and what does that mean for journalists and others who want to use it? By signing on to the services, the user agrees to their terms. But the language in those agreements may appear somewhat nebulous. *Twitter*'s terms of service, including *Periscope*, state that "What's yours is yours – you own your Content"

(2018). But, at the same time, when you agree to the terms, you grant them a "royalty-free license" that authorizes them "to make your Content available to the rest of the world and to let others do the same" (*Twitter* 2018).

Permitting others to use your content also appears in *Facebook*'s terms of service (for public posts). "When you publish content or information using the Public setting, it means that you are allowing everyone, including people off of Facebook, to access and use that information, and to associate it with you (i.e., your name and profile picture)" (*Facebook* 2018).

And on *YouTube*, "For clarity, you retain all of your ownership rights in your Content" (2018). Like other social media platforms, however, posting to the service also extends rights to others to use your content.

The Online News Association provides guidance on permission and credit for using others' content in its *Build Your Own Ethics Code* (ONA 2018). The most stringent would be the "permission first" approach, which would require permission before using any user-generated content. Less restrictive would be "use once verified." And in some cases, "factor in news value" would mean making exceptions for material that would produce significant journalism (ONA 2018).

Children and livestreaming

Children's privacy and protection from abuse has come to light as a crucial area for attention in livestreaming. In late autumn 2017, UK police arrested nearly 200 people suspected of child abuse – many of whom used livestreaming platforms in their crimes (NCA 2017). The National Crime Agency reports that predators capitalize on livestreaming's immediacy of contact and real-time comments. "Once on these platforms, offenders often use tricks or dares, the offer of online gifts or 'game points' and threats, in an attempt to manipulate young people into performing acts involving nudity over webcam" (NCA 2017).

The Children's Commissioner for England has called for compulsory digital literacy to be taught in primary schools (2018). In other countries, widespread abuse has prompted organizations like Unicef to work toward raising awareness and stopping these crimes (undated). But the potential for abuse extends beyond criminal exploitation of children's own use of livestreaming.

Emotional harm may be done inadvertently, by journalists and others who are streaming. In volatile situations, such as school shootings, interviewing child survivors can bring additional trauma to the students. Their proximity to the violence as well as their age can have an impact. The younger the child, the more likely there will be emotional complications (Simpson 2000).

After the 2007 Jokela school shooting in Finland, thousands signed a petition organized by the survivors, questioning the conduct of the media in covering the incident. Was it appropriate, it asked, to:

> stalk people with cameras at the entrance to the Crisis Centre; to pounce on hysterical people leaving the center, demanding a statement; to dig into the lives of the perpetrator and the victims to build a picture of a tragic life; or to secretly photograph people in their grief and publish the pictures without permission.
>
> (Finland Ministry of Justice 2009, 107)

A Finnish government study following the attack concluded that "being interviewed had a significant effect on post traumatic distress in traumatized adolescents" (Haravuori 2011, 75). Students may feel regret or even shame for giving interviews, and that may impede healing (Haravuori, Berg, and Marttunen 2017).

Those issues became apparent before the advent of social media, when live broadcasts were limited to television. Today, streaming live can introduce additional potential for misunderstanding. As journalists approach, will children and their families realize they're being livestreamed? As the Dart Center advised even before *Periscope* and *Facebook Live*, "Get permission before interviewing or photographing a child. Set clear ground rules about what is on and off the record. Don't talk down to a child. And don't make promises you can't keep" (Dart 2013).

It's imperative to state clearly that the interview is live, and on what platform. Keeping the child and family off camera while seeking permission provides some breathing room and affords the opportunity for them to refuse if they don't feel comfortable. The camera can instead stay on the crowd or another wide shot until permission is granted. Respecting children and their families can help guide livestreamers, not only in volatile situations, but in everyday settings as well.

Tech innovators take steps to address disruption

After journalists revealed that *Facebook* shared personal data for millions of people with the political data firm Cambridge Analytica (Granville 2018), lawmakers called Mark Zuckerberg to testify before the U.S. Senate and House of Representatives. But the issue of streaming live on social media was only mentioned once, in passing. Senator Cory Booker (2018) referenced the live broadcast of Philando Castile's killing on *Facebook*, in relation to police surveillance of organizations like Black Lives Matter.

In two days of testimony, the terms livestreaming/livestream/live stream were never used (*The Washington Post* 2018a, 2018b). Despite issues concerning live social broadcasts and children's safety, lawmakers chose not to probe them. Nor did they explore the pervasiveness of live video recording and its privacy implications. Instead, their questioning expanded beyond privacy to include censorship, liberal bias, and even diversity of *Facebook* employees. They even spent time on a "Fox-fueled" controversy about conservative bloggers Diamond & Silk.

Nonetheless, Zuckerberg announced action in the form of stepped-up security and content-review, with a total of 20,000 staff in this area by the end of 2018, and increased development and implementation of artificial intelligence (AI) tools. By imposing its own standards and self-regulation, *Facebook* may avoid government intervention, as did the film industry in 1930, with its Motion Picture Production Code (Shurlock 1947).

Other tech innovators hope to make change through raising public awareness. Tristan Harris, a former design ethicist at Google, has teamed up with others to "realign technology with humanity's best interests" (Center for Humane Technology 2018).

Harris says there's an invisible goal that drives technology in one direction – the "race to capture human attention" (Harris 2018).

And it's driven by a business model that equates money with our attention. Designers have been expert at creating apps and tools to attract and keep us engaged instead of empowering us, like auto-play videos, or the slot-machine action of pull-down refresh, to feed us more content (Harris 2017). One of the steps to taking control of our digital lives is through awareness. Harris and his team hope to create a cultural awakening to educate consumers about technology and attention.

Note

1 While *Facebook* had removed the livestreamed video, some of Robinson's other livestreams were still on the platform at the time of this writing. In one, he calls out Douglas Colson as a drug dealer. Colson became a suspect in the shooting, and the next day, turned himself in to police and was charged with first degree murder (Langone 2018).

References

Beckett, L. 2018. *Twitter*, August 26. https://twitter.com/loisbeckett/status/1033893760751419392

Booker, C. 2018. "Transcript of Mark Zuckerberg's senate hearing." *The Washington Post*, April 10. www.washingtonpost.com/news/the-switch/wp/2018/04/10/transcript-of-mark-zuckerbergs-senate-hearing/?utm_term=.95eaa793820d

Center for Humane Technology. 2018. Website. http://humanetech.com/

Chicago Tribune. 2018. "Facebook Live captures shooting of 2-year-old, 2 adults in Chicago." *Chicago Tribune*. www.chicagotribune.com/news/local/breaking/92579569-132.html

Children's Commissioner. 2018. "Life in 'likes': Children's Commissioner report into social media use among 8–12 year olds." *Children's Commissioner for England*. www.childrenscommissioner.gov.uk/wp-content/uploads/2018/01/Childrens-Commissioner-for-England-Life-in-Likes-3.pdf

Dart. 2013. "Interviewing children: Guidelines for journalists." *Dart Center for Journalism & Trauma*, January 31. https://dartcenter.org/content/interviewing-children-guide-for-journalists

Dockterman, E. 2016. "Snowden's Oliver Stone and Joseph Gordon-Levitt on Pokemon Go and surveillance." *Time*, July 21. http://time.com/4417714/snowden-movie-oliver-stone-pokemon-go/

Eordogh, F. 2018. "On demonetization and the YouTube shooter." *Forbes*, April 8. www.forbes.com/sites/fruzsinaeordogh/2018/04/08/on-demonetization-and-the-youtube-shooter/#5bb012137253

Facebook. 2016. "Report suicidal content." *Facebook*. www.facebook.com/help/contact/305410456169423

Facebook. 2018. "Terms of Service." *Facebook*, April 19. www.facebook.com/legal/terms

Finkelstein, H. 2018. In Rosenberg.

Finland Ministry of Justice. 2009. "Jokela School shooting on 7 November 2007: Report of the investigation commission." Ministry of Justice, Finland. https://schoolshooters.info/sites/default/files/Jokela%20School%20Shooting%20Official%20Report.pdf

Gingras, B. 2017. "Pennsylvania police open up about catching the 'Facebook killer'." *CNN*, May 12. www.cnn.com/2017/05/12/us/beyond-the-call-pennsylvania-police-catch-facebook-killer/

Godwin, R. 2016. In Hurst.

Gonzalez, E. 2018. *Twitter*, February 25. https://twitter.com/emma4change/status/967901935230693387

Granville, K. 2018. "Facebook and Cambridge analytica: What you need to know as fallout widens." *The New York Times*, March 19. www.nytimes.com/2018/03/19/technology/facebook-cambridge-analytica-explained.html

Grueskin, B. 2018. *Twitter*, June 28. https://twitter.com/BGrueskin/status/1012417311456849921

Gurman, S. 2016. "Terror talk changes as Comey refuses to name gunman." *Associated Press*, June 28. https://apnews.com/67d4fe9a88884794a79ffd464a8edc0b/terror-talk-changes-comey-refuses-name-gunman

Haravuori, H. 2011. "Effects of media exposure on adolescents traumatized in a school shooting." *Journal of Traumatic Stress*, 241: 70–77. https://onlinelibrary.wiley.com/doi/pdf/10.1002/jts.20605

Haravuori, H., Berg, N., and Marttunen, M. 2017. "The impact of journalism on grieving communities." In L. Wilson, Ed., *The Wiley Handbook of the Psychology of Mass Shootings*, pp. 170–187. West Sussex: John Wiley & Sons, Inc. https://books.google.com/books?hl=en&lr=&id=MEj4DAAAQBAJ&oi=fnd&pg=PA170&dq=journalism+children+privacy+&ots=Zvm8INRCPI&sig=bzIFHOuKOGUreOXRcSH_qFzyomY#v=onepage&q&f=false

Harris, T. 2017. "How a handful of tech companies control billions of minds every day." *Ted*, April. www.ted.com/talks/tristan_harris_the_manipulative_tricks_tech_companies_use_to_capture_your_attention

Harris, T. 2018. "Time well spent: Taking back our lives & attention." *Wisdom 2.0*. www.wisdom2summit.com/Videos/myriad_single_element/3274

Herron, R. 2017. "15-year-old boy live streams his suicide as part of dangerous viral 'blue whale challenge' that targets kids." *BET*, July 11. www.bet.com/news/national/2017/07/11/15-year-old-boy-live-streams-his-suicide-as-part-of-dangerous-vi.html

Hopkins, N. 2017. "Facebook will let users livestream self-harm, leaked documents show." *The Guardian*, May 21. www.theguardian.com/news/2017/may/21/facebook-users-livestream-self-harm-leaked-documents

Hurst, C. 2017. *Twitter*, April 16. https://twitter.com/ChrisHurstVA/status/853795288305328128

Inskeep, S. 2018. "Full transcript: Facebook COO Sheryl Sandberg on protecting user data." *NPR*, April 5. www.npr.org/2018/04/05/599761391/full-transcript-facebook-coo-sheryl-sandberg-on-protecting-user-data

Kasky, K. 2018. *Twitter*, May 30. https://twitter.com/cameron_kasky/status/1001938834823745538

Kissner, J. 2016. "Are active shootings temporally contagious? An empirical assessment." *Journal of Police and Criminal Psychology*, 311: 48–58. https://link.springer.com/article/10.1007/s11896-015-9163-8

Langone, A. 2018. "North Carolina Facebook Live murder suspect arrested." *People*, February 27. http://time.com/5178032/facebook-live-murder-suspect/

Lankford, A. and Madfis, E. 2018. "Don't name them, don't show them, but report everything else: A pragmatic proposal for denying mass killers the attention they seek and deterring future offenders." *American Behavioral Scientist*, 62(2): 260–279. http://journals.sagepub.com.ezproxy.wlu.edu/doi/abs/10.1177/0002764217730854

Lester, P. 2018. *Visual Ethics: A Guide for Photographers, Journalists, and Filmmakers*. New York: Routledge. www.taylorfrancis.com/books/9781315455129

Mann, T. 2017. "Woman saved just before committing suicide on Facebook Live." *Metro*, January 27. https://metro.co.uk/2017/01/27/woman-saved-just-before-committing-suicide-on-facebook-live-6410176/

McBride, K. 2017. "Don't call Steve Stephens 'The Facebook Killer'." *Poynter*, April 21. www.poynter.org/2017/dont-call-steve-stephens-the-facebook-killer/456868/

McCausland, P. 2017. "Memphis, Tennessee, man fatally sets himself on fire on Facebook Live." *NBC News*, May 14. www.nbcnews.com/news/us-news/memphis-tennessee-man-fatally-sets-himself-fire-facebook-live-n759366

Meindl, J. and Ivy, J. 2017. "Mass shootings: The role of the media in promoting generalized imitation." *American Journal of Public Health*, 1073: 368–370. http://dx.doi.org/10.2105/AJPH.2016.303611

Miller, C. and Burch, A. 2017. "Another girl hangs herself while streaming it live–this time in Miami." *Miami Herald*, January 24. www.miamiherald.com/news/local/article128563889.html

Morice, J. 2017. "Facebook killer chooses victim at random, laughs about killing in videos." *Cleveland.com*, April 18. www.cleveland.com/metro/index.ssf/2017/04/accused_facebook_live_killer_c.html

Mozur, P. 2017. "Father in Thailand kills 11-month-old daughter live on Facebook." *The New York Times*, April 25. www.nytimes.com/2017/04/25/world/asia/thailand-phuket-facebook-killing-daughter.html

NBC News. 2018. "Murder caught on Facebook Live." *NBC Nightly News with Lester Holt*, February 26. www.nbcnews.com/nightly-news/video/murder-caught-on-facebook-live-1171097155567

NCA. 2017. "245 children safeguarded and 192 arrests for child sex abuse offences." *National Crime Agency*, December 5. www.nationalcrimeagency.gov.uk/index.php/news-media/nca-news/1252-245-children-safeguarded-and-192-arrests-for-child-sex-abuse-offences

Nissenbaum, H. 2009. *Privacy in Context: Technology, Policy, and the Integrity of Social Life*. Stanford: Stanford University Press.

ONA. 2018. "User-generated content." *Online News Association, ONAethics*. https://ethics.journalists.org/topics/user-generated-content/

Pearce, M. 2018. *Twitter*, August 26. https://twitter.com/mattdpearce/status/1033884757703110656

Perez, C. 2018. "Man films his own murder." *Facebook* video posting. www.facebook.com/100023373335431/videos/174088423380268/

Periscope. 2018. "Community guidelines." www.periscope.tv/content

Remington, K. 2017. "Pennsylvania State Police talk about catching Cleveland Facebook killer." *Cleveland.com*, May 13. www.cleveland.com/metro/index.ssf/2017/05/pennsylvania_state_police_talk_1.html

Reporters Committee. Undated. "Immunity for reader comments under Section 230 of the Communications Decency Act." www.rcfp.org/browse-media-law-resources/digital-journalists-legal-guide/immunity-reader-comments-under-section-23

reporting on suicide.org. 2015. "Recommendations for reporting on suicide." http://reportingonsuicide.org/recommendations/#important

Roberts, M. 2018. "YouTube shooter fits the most important narrative of all." *The Washington Post*, April 5. www.washingtonpost.com/blogs/post-partisan/wp/2018/04/05/the-youtube-shooter-fits-the-most-important-narrative-of-all/?utm_term=.fb9f4982b1ef

Rosen, G. 2017. "Getting our community help in real time." *Facebook Newsroom*, November 27. https://newsroom.fb.com/news/2017/11/getting-our-community-help-in-real-time/

Rosenberg, E. 2018. "The Parkland shooting suspect has fans, and they're sending him letters and money." *The Washington Post*, March 29. www.washingtonpost.com/news/post-nation/wp/2018/03/28/the-parkland-shooter-has-fans-and-theyre-sending-him-letters-and-money/?utm_term=.b93696fd3b92

Rosenberg-Douglas, K. 2017. "Facebook Live assault of girl, 15: 'No one human deserves what happened to her'." *Chicago Tribune*, March 22. www.chicagotribune.com/news/local/breaking/ct-teen-girl-missing-from-lawndale-20170321-story.html

Sandberg, C. 2018. In Inskeep.

Schick, C. and Erdbrink, T. 2018. "Who was the YouTube shooter?" *The New York Times.* www.nytimes.com/video/world/middleeast/100000005833316/youtube-shooter-was-popular-and-ridiculed-in-iran.html

Schmadeke, S. 2017. "Teens in Facebook Live attack indicted, lawyers call case 'sensationalized'." *Chicago Tribune*, January 27. www.chicagotribune.com/news/local/breaking/ct-facebook-live-attack-court-met-20170127-story.html

Shear, M., Perez-Pena, R., and Blinder, A. 2015. "Ex-broadcaster kills 2 on air in Virginia shooting: Takes own life." *The New York Times*, August 26. www.nytimes.com/2015/08/27/us/wdbj7-virginia-journalists-shot-during-live-broadcast.html

Shurlock, G. 1947. "The motion picture production code." *The Annals of the American Academy of Political and Social Science*, 254: 140–146. www-jstor-org.ezproxy.wlu.edu/stable/1026152?seq=1#page_scan_tab_contents

Simpson, R. 2000. "Columbine: Interviewing children." *Dart Center for Journalism & Trauma*, April 20. https://dartcenter.org/content/columbine-interviewing-children

SPJ. 2014. "Code of Ethics." *Society of Professional Journalists*, September 6. www.spj.org/ethicscode.asp

Stewart, D. and Littau, J. 2016. "Up, periscope: Mobile streaming video technologies, privacy in public, and the right to record." *Journalism & Mass Communication Quarterly*, 932: 312–331. http://journals.sagepub.com/doi/abs/10.1177/1077699016637106

Stone, O. 2016. Quoted in Dockterman.

Towers, S., Gomez-Lievano, A., Khan, M., Mubayi, A., and Castillo-Chavez, C. 2015. "Contagion in mass killings and school shootings." *PLoS One* 10(7). http://journals.plos.org/plosone/article?id=10.1371/journal.pone.0117259

Twitter. 2018. "Twitter terms of service." *Twitter*, May 25. https://twitter.com/en/tos#update

twXplorer. 2017. "Knight lab." https://twxplorer.knightlab.com/

Unicef. Undated. "#ENDviolence online." *Unicef.* www.unicef.org/endviolence/endviolenceonline/

The Washington Post. 2018a. "Transcript of Mark Zuckerberg's senate hearing." *The Washington Post*, April 10. www.washingtonpost.com/news/the-switch/wp/2018/04/10/transcript-of-mark-zuckerbergs-senate-hearing/?utm_term=.95eaa793820d

The Washington Post. 2018b. "Transcript of Zuckerberg's appearance before House committee."April 11.www.washingtonpost.com/news/the-switch/wp/2018/04/11/transcript-of-zuckerbergs-appearance-before-house-committee/?utm_term=.878d5625261d

Yan, H. and Karimi, F. 2018. "YouTube shooter visited gun range before attacking strangers, police say." *CNN*, April 5. www.cnn.com/2018/04/04/us/youtube-hq-shooting/index.html

YouTube. 2018. "Terms of Service." *YouTube*, May 25. www.youtube.com/static?template=terms

Zuckerberg, M. 2017. *Facebook*, May 3. www.facebook.com/zuck/posts/10103695315624661

6 Monetization
Marvel meets menace

What happens when a social media giant offers news organizations millions of dollars to use its new product? They take it, and adopt the technology. Nearly 140 video creators accepted the offer from *Facebook* in 2016, with deals totaling more than $50 million. *CNN, The New York Times, BuzzFeed,* and others signed on to use *Facebook Live* for 12 months, beginning in March 2016 (Perlberg and Seetharaman 2016).

One year later, some of those companies had pared down their *Facebook Live* streams – cutting them in half, according to Columbia Journalism School's Tow Center research (Brown 2018). The livestreams appear to have dropped off after the incentive money ran out, prompting reactions such as "RIP Facebook Live" (Brown 2018). But, were the initial numbers realistic and sustainable, anyway? Reducing daily livestreams from four to two is not a likely harbinger of the platform's demise. Pressure to livestream by the numbers is equivalent to adopting the live-for-the-sake-of-live[1] television mindset. More doesn't necessarily equal better.

In fact, *The New York Times'* public editor argued at the time that *Facebook Live* was "too much, too soon" (Spayd 2016). "It's as if we passed over beta and went straight to bulk. What I hope is that *The Times* pauses to regroup, returning with a rigor that more sharply defines the exceptional and rejects the second-rate" (Spayd 2016).

Using livestreaming on social media to engage viewers in conversation around an issue or event, or to cover breaking stories as they unfold, can make better use of this story form. "We use it to interact with the audience, and we use it to engage the viewer directly," said Scott Wise of *WTVR* in Richmond, Virginia, in a report by the Knight Foundation (2018). The study found that nearly nine in ten television news directors did something new using social media in 2016, and for more than half, that included *Facebook Live* (Knight Foundation 2018). Many stations used the platform at least weekly, largely for breaking news and promoting journalists and on-air product. Some used it daily. *WLS-TV* in Chicago garnered nearly 70 million views for its 371 livestreams in 2016.

News managers not only cited the ability to draw viewers, but to serve them as well. "Any time a reporter is at breaking news, we stream. We know the phone is the first place people will see the story," said *KPLC* News Director Janelle Shriner in the Knight report (2018).

Facebook prioritized live video in its News Feed at about the same time it offered incentives to media companies.

> Facebook Live videos are more likely to appear higher in News Feed when those videos are actually live, compared to after they are no longer live. People spend more than 3x more time watching a Facebook Live video on average compared to a video that's no longer live.
>
> (Kant and Xu 2016)

The potential for pre-roll and embedded ads was palpable. In February 2017, *Facebook* made in-stream video ads available to eligible publishers reaching 300 or more concurrent viewers (Boland and Angelidou-Smith 2017).

Many media organizations view live broadcasting on social media largely through the lens of profitability. *CNN* executive Andrew Morse told *The Wall Street Journal* that monetization is a major consideration with livestreaming.

> Mr. Morse said that *CNN* would only continue to invest in such platforms if it sees a path to generating more revenue. "It's going to be hard for us to continue to do Facebook Live long-term if we can't figure out how to monetize it, because we're able to monetize our video really well in other places," he said.
>
> (Morse in Perlberg 2017)

In other words, corporate media operations that already make money placing their video elsewhere may perceive little financial incentive in adding another platform.

Doing more with less is also an issue, like cutting back on reporters in the field. Livestreaming pioneer and independent journalist Tim Pool says that this has interesting ramifications, that "because they've created a hole in the market by not showing up anymore, now, the people like us, are licensing that footage. So, now they end up having to pay for it anyway" (2018).

The profit motive in live broadcasting has been a driving force since its early days, reaching back to the development of the U.S. commercial radio model (Barnouw 1966). And even before that, criticism centered on material power and technological innovation. Instead of improving society, critics feared it would be used for enrichment (Smith and Marx 1994). That concern persists today with livestreaming on social media. And some unintended consequences have begun to materialize.

Live gaming and IRL livestreaming

Myriad live virtual worlds exist outside the news media and salient issues of the day. From live gaming on Amazon's *Twitch* to popular individuals broadcasting their daily lives, these livestreams attract millions. And for many, that means a handsome profit through subscription fees and product endorsements. With 140,000 subscribers on *Twitch*, Fortnite player Tyler "Ninja" Blevins earns upwards of a half-million dollars per month (Tassi 2018).

"Twitch is disrupting the traditional marketing model in the gaming industry," says Omeed Dariani, CEO at Online Performers Group (*CNBC* 2018). Now, gamers who stream on *Twitch* are "driving the conversation in an incredibly meaningful way" (Dariani in *CNBC* 2018).

Active *Twitch* broadcasters with large numbers of concurrent viewers can become partners, which provides additional revenue streams. That includes commercials, which the broadcaster can choose to run, including "how often they would like to run ads as well as how long the ads will last (between 30 and 180 seconds). For every 1000 advertisements served, the Partner will receive an industry-leading CPM" (*Twitch* 2017).

Some news organizations have *Twitch* channels, but as of this writing, their content has been fairly limited. *Buzzfeed News* livestreamed presidential election results from Mexico City (2018) and *The Washington Post* streamed five-plus hours of Mark Zuckerberg's testimony before Congress (2018).

Both channels included auto-play ads in their videos. On the playback, stats showed more than 150,000 viewers for the Mexico election, and fewer than 10,000 for each of the Zuckerberg testimony videos. It may still be too early to judge whether these news organizations can establish audiences via this mostly gaming platform.

Another model for monetization is IRL (in real life) broadcasting on *You-Tube*. Paul Denino, a.k.a. Ice Poseidon, makes a living by turning his life into a "self-produced reality show" (Chen 2018). If you open *YouTube* and search "ice," he pops up as one of the top offerings on the pull-down menu. With more than a half-million subscribers, sponsorships, and donations from viewers, the 23-year-old Denino said he was on track to make $60,000 in January 2018 (Chen 2018). But his publicly streamed life has gotten him "kicked out of six apartments" in Los Angeles since moving there less than two years ago. Swatting was a major problem – false reports called in to 911, leading to SWAT teams being sent out so the hoaxer could see it play out in real time (Chen 2018).

Disruptions such as these have made their way into public places via other IRL streamers. A "live streaming videoprank" on the University of Washington campus led to an arrest after a man walked into a room playing a recording announcing that a bomb was about to detonate (Peters 2018).

The suspect made money from donations to his YouTube channel via its "paid commenting system to play text-to-speech messages in public places," known as Super Chats (Baer 2018). Bail was set at $75,000 for Jammal Harraz, a.k.a. Arab Andy.

A *GoFundMe* page called "Save Arab Andy" was still active five months after the arrest. Set up by his manager to raise money for fees related to the incident, the site says, "Arab Andy is in jail and is unable to do so himself." It explains, "Arab Andy truly is harmless, and he never once made a threat. It was a YouTube video that one of his viewers chose to play over his speakers after making a donation." It also highlights this practice as a feature of his channel: "Viewers could donate a certain amount of money in exchange to play any YouTube video over his speakers for 30 seconds" (*GoFundMe* 2018).

But who is truly responsible – the person who provided the recording and paid to have it played, or the person who accepted money to play it in public? Or, are they both culpable? As these cases evolve, the courts will likely make that determination.

In the meantime, the UW video has been removed from Arab Andy's channels, but others remain. On May 31, 2018, Harraz broadcast live in downtown Seattle on his channel ISIS Poseidon. After getting on a bus, text appears briefly on the screen, "reptilehaus donated $4.20." Within the minute, as the bus stops and people approach the door to exit, a loud male voice on the stream shouts the N-word repeatedly. It appears to be coming from a speaker held by Arab Andy. After it stops, more text appears, and the shouting resumes. He exits the bus after a man behind him says, "You may think you have a freedom, and I do too. We all have freedoms. I'm just letting you know that you're gonna get what you're gonna get – crazy mother f*ers." The comments were all over the board, some goading Arab Andy to stay on the bus, others fearing the man was pulling a knife or gun, and even telling the streamer to run away (ISIS Poseidon 2018).

Are paid-commenting services contributing to extreme live video content? Yes, they are, says Joan Donovan, a researcher studying media manipulation for the New York City think tank, Data & Society. "When you stitch together broadcast and instant monetization, you get a behavior pattern that moves more and more toward extremes," she says (Donovan, quoted in Daro and Silverman 2018). Livestreams and live chats that can run for hours are difficult for *YouTube* to monitor, she notes.

And people are paying extremists using Super Chat to have their voices heard on livestreams. Neo-Nazis and white supremacists have profited from this formula. Super Chats on programs featuring Richard Spencer, Andy Warski, and Christopher Cantwell have generated thousands of dollars. Donovan says hateful comments can normalize those views through repetition, eventually becoming part of viewers' value systems (Donovan in Daro and Silverman 2018).

Chapter 7 delves further into live eyewitness video and its relation to perceptions of social issues, as well as the potential psychological impact of viewing and working with graphic content.

Note

1 The term "live-for-the-sake-of-live" refers to the overuse or misuse of live shots in television news. Positioning a reporter in front of an event location, hours after everyone's gone home, is one example of this practice. By using their expensive live broadcasting technology, stations attempt to justify those purchases.

References

Baer, S. 2018. "A YouTube livestreamer was arrested after making a prank bomb threat on a college campus." *BuzzFeed News*, June 2. www.buzzfeed.com/skbaer/youtube-arab-andy-arrested-bomb-threat?utm_term=.nh9r1aJNXG#.do2yYmagZz

Barnouw, E. 1966. *A Tower in Babel*. New York: Oxford University Press.

Boland, B. and Angelidou-Smith, M. 2017. "An update on video monetization." *Facebook for Media*, February 23. https://media.fb.com/2017/02/23/update-on-video-monetization/

Brown, P. 2018. "RIP Facebook live: As subsidies end, so does publisher participation." *Columbia Journalism Review*, February 23.

BuzzFeed News. 2018. "Left-wing populist Andrés Manuel López Obrador has won the Mexican Presidential Election." *Twitch*, July 1. www.twitch.tv/buzzfeednews

Chen, A. 2018. "Ice Poseidon's lucrative, stressful life as a live streamer." *The New Yorker*, July 9 & 16. www.newyorker.com/magazine/2018/07/09/ice-poseidons-lucrative-stressful-life-as-a-live-streamer

CNBC. 2018. "Twitch gamers are making six-figure salaries thanks to this . . ." *CNBC*, April 29. www.cnbc.com/video/2018/04/29/twitch-gamers-are-making-six-figure-salaries-thanks-to-this-mans-work-behind-the-scenes.html

Dariani, O. 2018. In *CNBC*.

Daro, I. and Silverman, C. 2018. "How YouTube's 'super chat' system is pushing video creators toward more extreme content." *BuzzFeed News*, May 17. www.buzzfeed.com/ishmaeldaro/youtube-comments-hate-speech-racist-white-nationalists-super?utm_term=.hyjZR0Je65#.stWyk5RvBe

Donovan, J. 2018. In Daro and Silverman.

GoFundMe. 2018. "Save Arab Andy." *GoFundMe*, June 2. www.gofundme.com/save-arab-andy

ISIS Poseidon. 2018. "Arab Andy in Downtown Seattle $3 TTS/$4.20 media." *You-Tube*, May 29. www.youtube.com/watch?v=0eP0JDNgfkg&feature=youtu.be

Kant, V. and Xu, J. 2016. "Taking into account live video when ranking feed." *Facebook Newsroom*, March 1. https://newsroom.fb.com/news/2016/03/news-feed-fyi-taking-into-account-live-video-when-ranking-feed/

Knight Foundation. 2018. "Local TV news and the new media landscape: Part 2, innovation and social media in local TV news." *Knight Foundation*, April 5. https://kf-site-production.s3.amazonaws.com/media_elements/files/000/000/170/original/TVNews2_InnovationAndSocialMedia_v4.pdf

Morse, A. 2017. In Perlberg.

Perlberg, S. 2017. "CNN's Andrew Morse talks network's plans for covering Donald Trump." *The Wall Street Journal*, January 4. www.wsj.com/articles/cnns-andrew-morse-talks-networks-plans-for-covering-donald-trump-1483551703

Perlberg, S. and Seetharaman, D. 2016. "Facebook signs deals with media companies, celebrities for Facebook live." *The Wall Street Journal*, June 22. www.wsj.com/articles/facebook-signs-deals-with-media-companies-celebrities-for-facebook-live-1466533472

Peters, L. 2018. "Man accused of broadcasting prank bomb threat at UW told to stay off YouTube." *KOMO News*, June 1. https://komonews.com/news/local/man-who-broadcast-prank-bomb-threat-at-uw-told-to-stay-off-youtube

Pool, T. 2018. "Antifa vs. far right: Front lines of the culture war." *Subverse*, August 21. www.youtube.com/watch?time_continue=32&v=ve53EJA0kHE

Shriner J. 2018. In Knight Foundation.

Smith, M. and Marx, L. 1994. *Does Technology Drive History? The Dilemma of Technological Determinism*. Cambridge: The MIT Press.

Spayd, L. 2016. "Facebook Live: Too much, too soon." *The New York Times*, August 20. www.nytimes.com/2016/08/21/public-editor/facebook-live-too-much-too-soon.html

Tassi, P. 2018. "'Fortnite' legend ninja talks twitch fame and fortune, and the game that got him there." *Forbes*, March 13. www.forbes.com/sites/insertcoin/2018/03/13/fortnite-legend-ninja-talks-twitch-fame-and-fortune-and-the-game-that-got-him-there/#5d737a8c45f7

Twitch. 2017. "Partner program overview." *Twitch*, October 6. https://help.twitch.tv/customer/en/portal/articles/735069-partner-program-overview

The Washington Post. 2018. "Zuckerberg testifies for second day on Capitol Hill." *Twitch*, April 11. www.twitch.tv/videos/249139876

Wise, S. 2018. In Knight Foundation.

7 Live eyewitness video

Psychological impact and issue perception

When horror and human suffering flow through social networks, distant witnesses often post their personal reactions to the images and sounds. Livestreams coming out of a church in Nicaragua caught the public's attention as pro-government groups shot at student protesters taking refuge there (*Al Jazeera* 2018).

Among the viewers, journalist Xeni Jardin tweeted,

> After listening to live, close-range gunfire & calm narration by a livestreamer inside the church, i couldn't sleep all night even when the feed went silent. I can't focus on anything today but those kids still trapped inside the church. #NicaraguaSOS.
>
> (Jardin 2018)

Jardin's reaction resonated with my own experience viewing livestreams for this book, especially the mass shooting in Parkland, Florida. I had been monitoring the story closely as it unfolded, finding it nearly impossible to go offline, and difficult to sleep. But the strongest physical response didn't come until the next morning. Feeling angry and sad, I'd been watching a live police update along with 37,000 viewers. I burst into tears when a woman on the stream said, "Having to tell (parents) . . . that a child, some 14 years old, is dead, is one of the hardest things you have to do in your career." Florida Attorney General Pam Bondi was describing the experience with victims' families who were waiting to hear about their children. "These parents, tremendous families, are grieving, and again, please respect their privacy" (Bondi 2018).

At that point, while watching a woman at a news conference, I envisioned *real* people who lost *real* children. Traumatic content can hit hard, with delayed reactions. I stepped away to give myself some time to regroup, and wondered how many journalists enmeshed in the content had to keep going to cover the story.

The previous night, the last tweet I read before trying to go to sleep was from journalist Ryan Broderick, who shared his personal experience working with traumatic content.

> Most of all, I recommend finding another reporter to go through this stuff with you. After MH17, @ellievhall and I found a Ukrainian hashtag people were using to post wreckage and bodies they were finding in their yards. We went through it in shifts. We talked through it.
>
> (Broderick 2018)

Note that MH17 is Malaysia Airlines Flight 17, the plane crash that killed 298 people after being shot down by a Russian-made missile (Walker 2018).

Studies suggest that frequent and extensive viewing of graphic, violent, non-fictional content is related to increased likelihood of psychological distress. In a study of journalists who worked with extremely violent user-generated images, researchers found that frequency was more distressing than duration (Feinstein, Audet, and Waknine 2014). The more frequently the journalists were exposed to the graphic images, the more likely they were to suffer from anxiety, depression, PTSD, or alcohol consumption.

Earlier research on viewing television coverage of the 9/11 World Trade Center terrorist attacks suggests a relationship between the length of time watched and greater likelihood of PTSD (Schlenger et al. 2002). Another study found similar results. Levels of PTSD and depression were higher among participants who repeatedly saw scenes of people falling or jumping from the towers (Ahern et al. 2002). Recall that social media and mobile viewing were not yet available during those attacks in 2001. Today, our phones and social media livestreaming allow for nearly unlimited viewing. We now carry those images with us, both cognitively and physically.

Knowing that violence is real appears to make a difference in viewers' reactions. Researchers showed participants scenes of actual violence or fictional violence. Those who knew they were watching real people being harmed responded with higher empathy than those who saw the fictional scenes (Ramos, Ferguson, Frailing, and Romero-Ramirez 2013). And, our past exposure to violence in real life can also play a role in our reactions. In another study, college students who had limited exposure to real-world violence had higher empathy, but those who had been exposed to violence in the real world had "higher trauma symptoms, escape to fantasy, and reduced empathy" (Mrug, Madan, Cook III, and Wright 2014, 1106). Taken together, these studies suggest a number of potential consequences for viewing violent imagery. The time spent viewing images of real-world violence and the frequency of viewing them can relate to our ability to empathize, and to negative psychological effects, including PTSD, depression, and anxiety.

As Broderick wrote,

> This isn't a sprint. Burn out is real. Reporting trauma from UGC is real. Take it easy. Know your limits. And if you're in newsrooms where you can't take breaks or work in tandem, find a few tools that work for you and use them.
>
> (2018)

The Dart Center for Journalism and Trauma offers suggestions for working with graphic images. Be mindful of your exposure "load," reduce unnecessary viewing, and build distance by avoiding faces and directing attention to other elements of the scene (2014).

Some find stepping away can help. Others move in more closely. Wesley Lowery, reporter for *The Washington Post*, covers policing and justice, and he writes that since covering Ferguson "it had been more or less my job to bear witness to pain and trauma" (2016, 224). In his book, *They Can't Kill Us All*, he writes that the most difficult video he's had to watch was the one livestreamed by Diamond Reynolds, showing her boyfriend, Philando Castile, dying after an officer had just shot him. "I sprang up from my desk and ran to the newsroom bathroom to throw up. Then I began reporting" (2016, 225). He notes that each of us copes with these deaths in different ways. "I escape by reporting," he writes. "Doing this keeps my mind busy. Often we all have an urge to 'do something.' For me, reporting is that something" (2016, 223).

And as we've seen throughout this book, "doing something" has taken many forms, from speaking out on livestreams to shutting down highways in protest.

Eyewitness video and our perceptions of social issues

While livestreaming delivers gripping scenes from human and natural disasters to our feeds, moments of joy and beauty also flow into that space. The royal wedding and solar eclipse coexist on live social media platforms along with police shootings and hurricanes.

How might seeing and sharing images from live eyewitness video fit with our perceptions of the world and issues that face us in our daily lives? Could they be related to our concerns and fears? The author's survey of more than 700 U.S. adults explores these questions.

The survey asked people about a number of key issues, such as racial unrest and climate change, and how concerned they were about them. It also asked if they had seen or shared specific eyewitness videos, like the Charlottesville attack and the March for Science. Then, for each issue, the analysis tested for different levels of concern between people who had and had not seen the eyewitness videos. (See Appendix 7.1 for detail on the research methods and findings.)

Concern about racial unrest

From summer 2016 to 2017, eyewitnesses livestreamed violent events related to race – among them, Philando Castile's death after a traffic stop outside Minneapolis, and the car attack that killed Heather Heyer after the Unite the Right rally in Charlottesville. Would concern about racial unrest be higher for people who saw these eyewitness videos? Yes; the findings show that their level of concern was higher compared to people who had not seen the videos. The difference was significant for both. Also, people who shared either of these videos on their social networks had higher levels of concern than those who did not share.

Concern about climate change

On Earth Day 2017, *Periscope* and *Facebook Live* brought the March for Science into viewers' feeds around the world. A few months later, Hurricane Harvey hit Texas, and people on the scene used the apps to livestream the storm, flooding, and rescues. Would people who saw the eyewitness video be more concerned about climate change than those who did not see the images? The findings were mixed. People who viewed the Science March did have higher levels of concern for climate change than those who did not. But there was no difference for Hurricane Harvey. Perhaps it was too soon for people to make the connection between the hurricane and climate change. Because the hurricane had hit Texas only two weeks before the survey was conducted, many of the respondents may still have been focused on the event itself rather than its larger, issue-based implications.

However, sharing did seem to make a difference. The results showed that those who shared eyewitness video of Hurricane Harvey on social media expressed greater concern about climate change than people who did not share. The same was found for sharing March for Science eyewitness video.

Concern about gun violence, terrorism, and safety in a public place

Five people died after a shooting at Florida's Fort Lauderdale airport in January 2017. Would people who saw eyewitness video be more concerned about gun violence, terrorism, and safety in a public place than those who did not? Yes; the findings showed differences for all three. Too few people shared video of the shooting, however, to test whether sharing was related to concern about the issues (fewer than 10 of the 700 respondents).

More on sharing eyewitness video

Other differences emerged when testing for sharing eyewitness video on social media. People who shared video of a van attack in Barcelona had higher concern for terrorism and for safety in public than those who did not share. And, those who shared eyewitness video of the 2017 Women's March were more concerned about healthcare and climate change than respondents who did not share.

More on watching eyewitness videos

On August 21, 2017, the moon passed between the sun and the earth, and 61 million people watched the phenomenon electronically (Miller 2017). Among them were the survey respondents. Out of about a dozen events, the solar eclipse was the most-watched on social media in real time. About one-fourth first saw it in a livestream. It was also the most-shared.

About half as many saw live eyewitness video of Hurricane Harvey in real time on *Periscope* or *Facebook Live*. It was the second-most-shared video in the study.

Some of the survey-takers had a daily dose of live social video. Nearly one-third said they spent some time every day watching *Periscope* or *Facebook Live*. And, almost every person surveyed recalled seeing eyewitness video from at least one recent event (less than one percent said they hadn't).

Some eyewitness video reached more viewers on social media *after* it happened, such as Chewbacca Mom, the 2017 Women's March, and Philando Castile. And some was first seen by more viewers on news *outside* social media, such as Hurricane Harvey and the Barcelona van attack.

More on the issues

The study participants reported the greatest concern about healthcare. This finding tracks closely with a Gallup poll (2017) that showed healthcare among the top issues facing the country at that time.

Climate change ranked second for people in this study, and the third was a tie among gun violence, racial unrest, and loss of freedom.

Discussion: what might these findings mean?

The research suggests a relationship between viewing live eyewitness video and our perceptions of the world and issues that face us in our daily lives. People who saw certain eyewitness video had significantly greater concern for some issues than those who had not. This was supported for racial unrest, climate change, gun violence, terrorism, and safety in a public place. It's important to note that while viewers had higher levels of concern for these issues, the study did not test for causation. Nonetheless, having seen these videos appeared to be a factor in relation to the issue concern.

Kelly's concept of *flow* (2016), introduced in Chapter 1, can offer insight into these results. Recall that digital manipulability plays a key role in *flow*, and that livestreams can be saved as videos, audios, and screenshots, and can be clipped, shared, and linked. In other words, they are highly manipulable, which enhances *flow*. While not everyone turns to *Periscope* or *Facebook Live* to watch in real time, they do see pieces of livestreams in other forms – on social networks or other media platforms. This was evident in the findings. Eyewitness videos first reached some viewers in real time, and others on social networks or in news outside social media. In their many forms, livestreams become part of our cultural storytelling, relating to our concern about the issues surrounding those images.

Sharing this content also contributes to the *flow* and appears related to people's perception of social issues. Those who shared eyewitness video had higher levels of concern for racial unrest, climate change, terrorism, and safety in public places.

In addition to *flow*, a number of factors at play in shaping attitudes could include the people in your social networks, the role of push notifications, and news consumption habits. Further studies might draw from work on opinion leaders, agenda setting, and cultivation theory.

References

Ahern, J., Galea, S., Resnick, H., Kilpatrick, D., Bucuvalas, M., Gold, J., and Vlahov, D. 2002. "Television images and psychological symptoms after the September 11 terrorist attacks." *Psychiatry: Interpersonal and Biological Processes*, 654: 289–300. http://guilfordjournals.com/doi/abs/10.1521/psyc.65.4.289.20240

Al Jazeera. 2018. "Nicaragua unrest: Student protester livestreams attack." *Al Jazeera*, July 14. www.aljazeera.com/news/2018/07/nicaragua-unrest-student-protester-livestream-attack-180714060224118.html

Bondi, P. 2018. "Police give an update on the Florida school shooting that has left at least 17 people dead." *BuzzFeed News* livestream on *Periscope*, February 15. www.pscp.tv/w/1YpKkEReZPrJj?q=buzzfeed+news

Broderick, R. 2018. *Twitter*, February 14. https://twitter.com/broderick/status/963978874643103744

Casler, K., Bickel, L., and Hackett, L. 2013. "Separate but equal? A comparison of participants and data gathered via Amazon's MTurk, social media, and face-to-face behavioral testing." *Computers in Human Behavior*, 29(6): 2156–2160. www.sciencedirect.com/science/article/pii/S074756321300160X

Clifford, S., Jewell, R., and Waggoner, P. 2015. "Are samples drawn from Mechanical Turk valid for research on political ideology?" *Research & Politics*, 2: 4. http://journals.sagepub.com/doi/abs/10.1177/2053168015622072

Dart Center. 2014. "Working with traumatic imagery." *Dart Center*, August 12. https://dartcenter.org/content/working-with-traumatic-imagery

Feinstein, A., Audet, B., and Waknine, E. 2014. "Witnessing images of extreme violence: A psychological study of journalists in the newsroom." *Journal of the Royal Society of Medicine Open*, 58: 1–7. http://journals.sagepub.com/doi/full/10.1177/2054270414533323

Gallup. 2017. "Most important problem." August. http://news.gallup.com/poll/1675/most-important-problem.aspx

Hauser, D. and Schwarz, N. 2015. "Attentive Turkers: MTurk participants perform better on online attention checks than do subject pool participants." *Behavior Research Methods*, 48(1): 400–407. https://link.springer.com/article/10.3758/s13428-015-0578-z

Jardin, X. 2018. *Twitter*, July 14. https://twitter.com/xeni/status/1018171768547266561

Kelly, K. 2016. *The Inevitable: Understanding the 12 Technological Forces That Will Shape Our Future*. New York, NY: Penguin Books.

Lowery, W. 2016. *They Can't Kill Us All: Ferguson, Baltimore, and a New Era in America's Racial Justice Movement*. New York: Little, Brown and Company.

Miller, J. 2017. "Americans and the 2017 Eclipse: An initial report on public viewing of the August total solar eclipse." September 21. www.isr.umich.edu/cps/initialeclipseviewingreport.pdf

Mrug, S., Madan, A., Cook III, E., and Wright, R. 2014. "Emotional and physiological desensitization to real-life and movie violence." *Journal of Youth and Adolescence*, 445: 1092–1108. https://link.springer.com/article/10.1007/s10964-014-0202-z

Pickett, J. and Baker, T. 2014. "The pragmatic American: Empirical reality or methodological artifact?" *Criminology*, 52(2): 195–222. http://onlinelibrary.wiley.com/doi/10.1111/1745-9125.12035/abstract

Ramos, R., Ferguson, C., Frailing, K., and Romero-Ramirez, M. 2013. "Comfortably numb or just yet another movie? Media violence exposure does not reduce viewer empathy for victims of real violence among primarily Hispanic viewers." *Psychology of Popular Media Culture*, 21: 2–10. http://psycnet.apa.org/journals/ppm/2/1/2/

Schlenger, W., Caddell, J., Ebert, L., Jordan, B., Rourke, K., Wilson, D., Thalji, L., Dennis, J., Fairbank, J., and Kulka, R. 2002. "Psychological reactions to terrorist attacks Findings from the National Study of Americans' reactions to September 11." *JAMA*, 2885: 581–588. http://jamanetwork.com/journals/jama/fullarticle/195165

Smith, S., Roster, C., Golden, L., and Albaum, G. 2016. "A multi-group analysis of online survey respondent data quality: Comparing a regular USA consumer panel to MTurk samples." *Journal of Business Research*, 69(8): 3139–3148. www.sciencedirect.com/science/article/pii/S014829631500627X

Walker, S. 2018. "MH17 downed by Russian military missile system, say investigators." *The Guardian*, May 24. www.theguardian.com/world/2018/may/24/mh17-downed-by-russian-military-missile-system-say-investigators

Appendix 7.1

Methods and key findings for live eyewitness video and perceptions of social issues

Data were collected on September 8, 2017, through an online survey of U.S. adults via Amazon MTurk. The validity of MTurk samples and data has been supported through numerous studies (Clifford, Jewell, and Waggoner 2015; Casler, Bickel, and Hackett 2013; Hauser and Schwarz 2015). In line with recommendations for valid responses, the present survey restricted participation to a U.S. population (Smith, Roster, Golden, and Albaum 2016). And, as a quality check, questionnaires completed in less than two minutes were disqualified, yielding 711 valid questionnaires.

The instrument included a series of questions to measure perceptions of social issues using a five-point Likert scale. Phrasing varied to help protect against acquiescence bias (Pickett and Baker 2014). Examples of questions follow:

Note how much you agree or disagree with the following statements:

- *It's safe to walk alone in my neighborhood during the day*
- *Global climate change caused by human activities is occurring now*

How concerned are you about:

- *Your own safety in a public place*
- *Racial unrest*
- *Climate change*
- *Terror attacks*

Exposure was measured for 11 eyewitness videos, defined as:

People have been using their phones to make videos from wherever they happen to be (eyewitness video). Where did you first see the following eyewitness video?

Examples of eyewitness videos were drawn from citizen livestreams that had been made during 2016 and 2017. Each question included a brief description of the video, for example: "Charlottesville car attack that killed protester Heather Heyer," and "Hurricane Harvey (Texas storm/flooding)." The presentation order alternated non-violent and violent examples.

Detail on participant exposure to each video was collected. For example:

Where did you first see eyewitness video of the March for Science on Earth Day?

- *Facebook Live or Periscope as it was happening*
- *Social media after it happened*
- *News report outside social media*
- *I don't recall where I saw it*
- *I did not see eyewitness video of this*

Media exposure in general was measured by asking:

On a typical day, how much time do you spend:

- *using social media*
- *watching video*
- *playing video games*
- *consuming news*
- *watching Periscope or Facebook Live?*

Demographic data included gender (45 percent women, 55 percent men), age (18–20 through 70–79, with most aged 30–39), education (43 percent college graduates), and race/ethnicity (76 percent white/Caucasian, 9 percent black/African American, 7 percent Asian/Asian American, 6 percent Hispanic/Latino).

Viewing eyewitness video and concern about racial unrest

An independent-samples t-test was conducted to compare levels of concern about racial unrest between people who did and did not see eyewitness video of the:

- Charlottesville attack. There was a significant difference in levels of concern for people who saw (M=3.26, SD=1.16) and did not see the video (M=2.93, SD=1.23); t=(−2.89); p = .004.
- Diamond Reynolds video of Philando Castile. There was a significant difference in levels of concern for people who saw (M=3.34, SD=1.19) and did not see the video (M=3.06, SD=1.16); t=(−3.15); p = .002.

Viewing eyewitness video and concern about climate change

An independent-samples t-test was conducted to compare levels of concern about climate change between people who did and did not see eyewitness video of the March for Science. There was a significant difference in levels of concern for people who saw (M=3.78, SD=1.25) and did not see the video (M=3.26, SD=1.31); t=(−5.24); p = .000.

Viewing eyewitness video and concern about gun violence, terrorism, and safety in a public place

An independent-samples t-test was conducted to compare levels of concern for these issues between people who did and did not see eyewitness video of the Ft. Lauderdale airport shooting.

- *Gun violence*: There was a significant difference in levels of concern for people who saw (M=3.31, SD=1.20) and did not see the video (M=3.04, SD=1.26); t=(−2.92); p = .004.
- *Terrorism*: There was a significant difference in levels of concern for people who saw (M=3.04, SD=1.21) and did not see the video (M=2.63, SD=1.20); t=(−4.53); p = .000.
- *Safety*: There was a significant difference in levels of concern for people who saw (M=2.92, SD=1.07) and did not see the video (M=2.69, SD=1.11); t=(−2.76); p = .006.

Sharing eyewitness video and concern about racial unrest

An independent-samples t-test was conducted to compare levels of concern about racial unrest between people who did and did not share eyewitness video of the:

- Charlottesville attack. There was a significant difference in levels of concern for people who shared (M=3.69, SD=1.22) and did not share the video (M=3.17, SD=1.17); t=(−2.70); p = .007.
- Diamond Reynolds video of Philando Castile. There was a significant difference in levels of concern for people who shared (M=4.16, SD=1.18) and did not share the video (M=3.17, SD=.83); t=(−3.62); p = .000.

Sharing eyewitness video and concern about climate change

An independent-samples t-test was conducted to compare levels of concern about climate change between people who did and did not share eyewitness video of:

- March for Science. There was a significant difference in levels of concern for people who shared (M=4.42, SD=.81) and did not share the video (M=3.44, SD=1.31); t=(−3.80); p = .000.
- Hurricane Harvey. There was a significant difference in levels of concern for people who shared (M=3.80, SD=1.23) and did not share the video (M=3.42, SD=1.32); t=(−2.83); p = .005.
- 2017 Women's March. There was a significant difference in levels of concern for people who shared (M=4.42, SD=.85) and did not share the video (M=3.41, SD=1.31); t=(−5.25); p = .000.

Sharing eyewitness video of the Barcelona van attack and concern about safety in a public place

There was a significant difference in levels of concern for people who shared (M=3.33, SD=.97) and did not share the video (M=2.78, SD=1.10); t=(−2.30); p = .020.

Sharing eyewitness video of the 2017 Women's March and concern about healthcare

There was a significant difference in levels of concern for people who shared (M=4.19, SD=.84) and did not share the video (M=3.78, SD=1.07); t=(−2.59); p = .010.

8 Ball of confusion

Sorting out livestream disruptions[1]

As summer fades, #NeverAgain persists. Parkland survivors continue rallying against gun violence and registering young voters across the country. David Hogg's *Periscope* from a Chicago protest garners 88,000 viewers, up exponentially from about 500 for his live broadcast outside Stoneman Douglas High School five months earlier (2018). And in August, the activists demonstrate outside NRA headquarters in Washington, D.C., as livestreams keep these events in the public eye (TicToc 2018).

In this final chapter we revisit the potential of live social video to disrupt – both negatively, and as a positive force for change. The NRA protest and two other events that unfolded on the same day illustrate some of these disruptions, as do examples reintroduced from earlier chapters.

Real-time distant witnessing

While the streams coming out of D.C. convey a mostly peaceful demonstration, live broadcasts from Portland, Oregon reveal a charged confrontation. Some of the video producers that appear throughout this book are in the midst of the crowd, streaming live on social media as police in riot gear hold off right-wing marchers and anti-fascist protesters. Ford Fischer, Unicorn Riot, and Tim Pool join Portland reporters and others in the thick of the action. Members of the far-right group Patriot Prayer and counter-protesters stream with their phones. "I'm always surprised by just how many people show up to livestream these things," notes a local journalist (Campuzano 2018a). Alex Jones' *InfoWars* is also streaming, days before *Facebook* and *YouTube* shut down his pages and accounts, citing violations for glorifying violence and hate speech (Nicas 2018).

I watch along with thousands of distant witnesses as police shoot flash bang grenades and tear gas to disperse the civil disturbance. Soon, questions about the action emerge, and the livestreams offer some insight into what is unfolding. In one, *KATU* television reporter Lashay Wesley flinches as a deafening bang goes off. Maintaining a professional composure, she hustles out of frame, explaining, "We're trying to move west because Portland Police have just used some items to get the crowd to move away." Two loud shots follow (*KATU* 2018). At about the same time, journalist Eder Campuzano cuts off his *Facebook* stream for *The Oregonian* after getting hit on the head during the "fracas." He said he was not targeted, but was "in the wrong place at the wrong time" when he was hit by what he thought was a water bottle (Campuzano 2018b). The stream ends abruptly just as he says a painful, "God . . ." (*Oregonian* 2018).

Others are injured, and Oregon's American Civil Liberties Union calls on Portland police to stop using excessive force against protesters (ACLU 2018). Police then suspend the use of flash bang grenades while they investigate (Shepherd 2018).

Credibility, truth telling, and transparency

Live videos from the scene in Portland and elsewhere exemplify what Peters calls access to truth and authenticity (2001). Trained journalists along with honest observers and participants document events as they unfold, in-person, on-location. This transparency reveals the process as it evolves. But there are barriers. Some may inadvertently gravitate toward something while missing key events. Others may purposely mislead through their narrations, or even manipulate by orchestrating or avoiding action. Nonetheless, credible, real-time social witnessing via livestream can make a difference. "You don't have to be left-wing or anti-anybody," says independent journalist and livestreamer Ford Fischer. "By just livestreaming you just show the thing that happens, and subject them to all the criticism or consequences that come from that" (2018).

A force for change

Livestreams deliver powerful images and sounds, like police in riot gear moving aggressively, blasting flash bang grenades, and pepper spraying protesters. Documenting violence in real time through numerous streaming video sources can provide evidence to support change or propel people to act. The many versions of an event streamed on-site by multiple eyewitnesses can help illuminate truth. And in some cases, a single livestream can have a profound impact, like Diamond Reynolds' *Facebook Live* broadcast as Philando Castile lay dying. Even inaction, like a senator being denied entrance to an immigrant detention facility, can spark outrage and galvanize.

Collective emboldening

#NeverAgain brought teens and adults together for change. Their collective energy helped propel their movement toward the 2018 midterm elections. In August, the teens joined forces with the NAACP to register young voters (2018). Along the way, livestreams played a role in bringing the movement to light and emboldening others to act. Students left their classrooms during the National School Walkout to support stricter gun laws – some going solo – having seen others do so and being empowered to take a stand (Murphy and Mezzofiore 2018).

But collective emboldening can also disrupt to harm. Streaming platforms that spread hate and violence can contribute to normalizing the language, behaviors, and groups that proliferate them. While some are being removed for violating social media policies, others persist.

Challenges and conveniences for journalists

As I watched reporters broadcasting live from Portland, I worried for their safety. Some wore protective gear, but others did not, including *The Oregonian's* Campuzano. After being hit, he tweeted, "Coulda used that headgear about an hour ago. Live and learn, I guess!" (2018c).

In addition to personal safety, streaming in the field imposes many other demands, including logistics, gear, and interacting with viewers. Managing all of this while operating solo is often the norm for streaming journalists.

Live broadcasts on social media also bring conveniences, such as the availability of citizen eyewitness video, which can allow news media to take viewers to breaking events without sending out their own crews. However, Zelizer warns that content from private citizens can sometimes give the illusion that journalists are on the scene (Zelizer 2007).

Interactivity, engagement, and a forum for discussion

One of the hallmarks of interactive digital media has been the potential for engaging with citizens around issues and events. That forum for discussion during livestreams can involve journalists and viewers in productive democratic dialogue, moving the reporting away from simply a unidirectional lecture, toward what Kovach and Rosensteil call journalism as service (2010). And as the *CBC* has done with its interactive *Facebook Live* newscasts, the platform provides a story form that brings additional content to the broadcast, for greater depth and conversation with viewers.

Also, with many news organizations shutting down their comment sections, livestreaming offers an alternative forum for discussion. Granted, trolls can impede civil discourse during streams by posting distasteful, hateful, or even violent comments. And as social media platforms respond to "bad actors" by removing accounts that facilitate such speech, we may find fewer livestreamers willing to keep comments open during their broadcasts.

Amplification, spreading negativity, and hate

As the Portland protesters disperse, Trump TV is streaming its namesake on *YouTube* as he gives a speech in a hot Ohio gymnasium. His caustic criticism attacks politicians and news media. "Maxine Waters . . . Maxine. A seriously low-IQ person. Seriously." And *CNN*. "They're so dishonest. These are among the most dishonest human beings you will ever meet. . . . These are really bad people" (Trump TV 2018).

The hateful messages are amplified as news outlets stream the speech on their own sites. For television networks, no preempting of regular programming is needed, as viewers can find the stream on their mobile devices, fed to them via notifications on social networks, or showcased as featured broadcasts. Savvy social media teams that know how to game algorithms or use other means may successfully drive their content to the top or become featured feeds.

Monetization

Balancing the power of technology for human betterment versus the drive for profit dates back to at least the Industrial Revolution. At that time, Benjamin Franklin refused to patent his inventions to enrich himself, viewing them, instead, as a way to serve others (Smith and Marx 1994). Today, tech companies pay content producers to use their products, imposing financial and technological leverage that some critics view as worrisome (Rein and Venturini 2018). And for livestreaming, there's also the business model fueled by advertising.

Ads that appear before, during, and after live broadcasts can bring revenue to both the hosting platform and the streamer. Many would consider that a positive disruption that supports free content. One might call into question, though, the ethics of elected officials enriching themselves or their campaigns financially through ads in these live videos. Trump's Ohio *YouTube* broadcast includes numerous ads throughout the playback. In addition, his stream features Super Chats, a means to monetize as he speaks. Viewers pay to have their comments displayed prominently in the broadcast in real time. A $100 payment funded the message "TRUMP!! MAGA!!" in a red box at the top of the comment feed, along with the name Deplorable Dee (Trump TV 2018).

The concept of paying to be heard goes beyond monetization, as we've seen with the IRL (in-real-life) streamers. In the most extreme cases, viewers pay streamers to broadcast offensive messages and can result in criminal behaviors, like the bomb scare in Seattle.

Violence and its impact

Graphic, horrifying images, livestreamed both accidentally and intentionally, invade our screens. They can bring a multitude of potential effects, from pain, trauma, and contagion, to outrage and action. Earlier chapters explore these issues in detail.

Privacy and protecting children

Our ability to broadcast live, basically anywhere, anytime, is both liberating and invasive. Along with its brilliance, this technological innovation has also revealed the dark side of human nature.

Our right to privacy, and safety for children, can be challenged through this disruption. While some countries have instituted policies to monitor and protect, much of this space is unregulated and can be an environment for exploitation of minors.

Flow and issue perception

As we've seen throughout this book, the events and issues on our digital screens do not unfold in a vacuum. We've explored how the *flow* facilitates our experience with live social media video. Yes, we can view the unfiltered images from an eyewitness who is streaming on *YouTube* in real time. But, the more likely scenario involves digital manipulation, which can deliver myriad content options, from a sound bite in our feed to a photo on a newspaper's front page.

These many paths to seeking truth become part of the *flow* that contributes to our cultural storytelling. Early research points to a relationship between viewing eyewitness live video and our perceptions of social issues – from concern about racial unrest and gun violence to climate change. (See Chapter 7 for further details.)

Moving forward: The human connection

The technological determinist would argue that livestreaming tools themselves drive our social and cultural development. Granted, without the innovation, the impact would be moot – there would be no streams. But, returning to the live video explored throughout this book, example after example points to the human connection at the heart of this technology – eyewitnesses, journalists, protesters, politicians, viewers, and more. Reflecting on his pioneering livestreams during the 2015 Baltimore riots, journalist Paul Lewis stressed the human aspect of livestreaming. As always, "the stories are about people" (Lewis, in Artwick 2018).

The value of this human connection can get clouded amidst the negative disruptions of the technology, from its addictive nature to the drive for profit. Awareness of these competing forces is a first step in moving toward the positive disruptions they can bring, while curtailing the potential to "hijack" society. Striving for such a cultural awakening, technology ethicist Tristan Harris says, "I want to live in a world where the tech industry is actually about helping humanity" (2018). So too, with social media livestreaming, driving disruption as a positive force for change.

Note

1 "Ball of Confusion" by the Temptations tackles the social ills and mood of the nation in 1970, but its lyrics and hip-hop style delivery are apropos to today's disruptions (Newseum 2015). The song was performed and livestreamed at *A Concert for Charlottesville*, after the violence that killed protester Heather Heyer.

References

ACLU. 2018. "ACLU of Oregon comment on the Portland Police Bureau's response to protest." *ACLU Oregon*, August 6. www.aclu-or.org/en/press-releases/aclu-oregon-comment-portland-police-bureaus-response-protest

Artwick, C. 2018. "Social media livestreaming." In S. Eldridge II & B. Franklin, Eds., *The Routledge Handbook of Developments in Digital Journalism Studies*. Abingdon: Routledge.

Campuzano, E. 2018a. *Twitter*, August 4. https://twitter.com/edercampuzano/status/1025837665168449536

Campuzano, E. 2018b. "OPINION: I'm the reporter you saw bleeding at the Portland protests; here's my story." *The Oregonian*, August 7. www.oregonlive.com/opinion/index.ssf/2018/08/im_the_reporter_you_saw_bleeding_at_portland_protests.html

Campuzano, E. 2018c. *Twitter*, August 4. https://twitter.com/edercampuzano/status/1025868292395651072

Fischer, F. 2018. "Antifa vs. far right: Front lines of the culture war." *Subverse*, August 21. www.youtube.com/watch?time_continue=32&v=ve53EJA0kHE

Harris, T. 2018. "Tristan Harris says tech companies have opened Pandora's Box." *Bloomberg*, January 17. www.bloomberg.com/news/videos/2018-01-18/tristan-harris-says-tech-companies-have-opened-pandora-s-box-video

Hogg, D. 2018. "Registering counter protesters to vote." *Periscope*, July. www.pscp.tv/w/1zqJVLnVjLLKB?q=david+hogg

KATU. 2018. "LIVE: Dueling protests kick off in Portland." *KATU*, August 4. www.facebook.com/katunews/videos/10155907697921448/

Kovach, B. and Rosenstiel, T. 2010. *Blur: How to Know What's True in the Age of Information Overload.* New York: Bloomsbury USA.

Lewis, P. 2018. In Artwick.

Murphy, P. and Mezzofiore, G. 2018. "At a school in North Carolina, he was the only one of 700 students who walked out." *CNN*, March 15. www.cnn.com/2018/03/14/us/student-walks-out-alone-trnd/index.html

NAACP. 2018. "March for our lives tour joins NAACP in digital voter registration drive." *NAACP*, August 6. www.naacp.org/latest/march-lives-tour-joins-naacp-digital-voter-registration-drive/

Newseum. 2015. "Vietnam music Monday: Ball of confusion." *Newseum*, November 23. www.newseum.org/2015/11/23/vietnam-music-monday-ball-of-confusion/

Nicas, J. 2018. "Alex Jones and infowars content is removed from Apple, Facebook and YouTube." *The New York Times*, August 6. www.nytimes.com/2018/08/06/technology/infowars-alex-jones-apple-facebook-spotify.html

Oregonian. 2018. "The Oregonian was live." *Facebook Live*, August 4. www.facebook.com/theoregonian/videos/10156017949956973/

Peters, J. 2001. "Witnessing." *Media, Culture & Society*, 236: 707–723. http://journals.sagepub.com/doi/10.1177/016344301023006002

Rein, K. and Venturini, T. 2018. "Ploughing digital landscapes: How Facebook influences the evolution of live video streaming." *New Media & Society*, January 6.

Shepherd, K. 2018. "Portland Police suspend use of 'flash-bang' grenades after reports that several protesters were severely injured by the weapons." *Willamette Week*, August 6. www.wweek.com/news/courts/2018/08/06/portland-police-suspend-use-of-flash-bang-grenades-after-reports-that-several-protesters-were-severely-injured-by-the-weapons/

Smith, M. and Marx, L. 1994. *Does Technology Drive History? The Dilemma of Technological Determinism.* Cambridge: The MIT Press.

TicToc. 2018. "HAPPENING NOW: 'National march on the NRA' rally outside National Rifle Association headquarters #tictocnews." *Periscope*, August 4. www.pscp.tv/w/1OdJrpNqkgnKX?q=nra

Trump TV. 2018. "LIVE: President Donald Trump MASSIVE rally in Lewis Center, Ohio–August 4, 2018." *YouTube*, August 4. www.youtube.com/watch?v=Ii-xurtnfS4

Zelizer, B. 2007. "On 'having been there': 'Eyewitnessing' as a journalistic key word." *Critical Studies in Media Communication*, 245: 408–428. www.tandfonline.com/doi/abs/10.1080/07393180701694614

Index

100   *Index*